TRIBAL FOOD HABITS

TRIBAL FOOD HABITS

P. Rajyalakshmi

GIAN PUBLISHING HOUSE
New Delhi-110002

TRIBAL FOOD HABITS
(Tribal Studies, Home Science)

ISBN: 81-212-0337-6

Published in 1999 in India by
Gyan Publishing House
5, Ansari Road
New Delhi-110002

Printed at Goyal Offset Printers, Delhi.

ACKNOWLEDGEMENTS

The author expresses her immense gratitude to

Dr. (Mrs.) P. Geervani, Prof. and Head, Department of Foods and Nutrition, College of Home Science, Andhra Pradesh Agricultural University, for her invaluable guidance, encouragement and help throughout the period of the study.

She is extremely grateful to Dr. Ramastry, Deputy Director (Retd.) Department of Analytical Chemistry, National Institute of Nutrition, Indian Council of Medical Research, Hyderabad, for his timely guidance, help and assistance in planning and carrying out the research work.

She is indebted to Dr. (Mrs.) P. Pushpamma, Dean of Home Science Faculty, Andhra Pradesh Agricultural University for providing all facilities for conducting the research work and for her valuable suggestions.

She expresses her thanks to Dr. (Mrs.) K.Chttemma Rao, Principal, College of Home Science, Andhra Pradesh Agricultural University, for her valuable help.

She is immensely thankful to the Block Development offcers and extension staff of the two blocks for providing help and accommodation during the stay. Special thanks are due to Smt. Mangayamma, Smt. Kantamma and Sri. Trinadh Rao for their untiring help and assistance during the field work.

She wishes to express her thanks to the Director and Staff of Tribal Cultural Research and Training Institue, Tribal Welfare Department, Hyderabad, for their help and for allowing her to avail of the library facilities.

She is thankful to all the staff of College of Home Science for their help and encouragement.

She is thankful to Sri Madhava Rao, Asst. Professor, Department of Plant Breeding, APAU, for helping in the identification of the uncommon foods.

She is also thankful to the freelance photographer Mr. Prakash Sharma and Mr. Srinivas, the typist for their timely help and co-operation.

She is extremely grateful to her parents for being understanding and encouraging all through the research period.

She is grateful to the Andhra Pradesh Agricultural University for giving an opportunity by deputation for Ph.D.

Last but not the least she is thankful to ICAR for providing senior fellowship, for a perod of three and half years of her study.

P. Rajyalakshmi

CONTENTS

ABBREVIATONS

AICRP	All India Co-ordinated Research Project
AIU	Amylase Inhibitor Units
AOAC	Association of Official and Agricultural Chemists
CHS	College of Home Science
ICMR	Indian Council of Medical Research
IVPD	*In vitro* protein digestibility
IVSD	*In vitro* starch digestibility
NIN	National Institute of Nutrition
NNMB	National Nutrition Monitoring Bureau
NRC	Nutrition Research Cell
PAG	Protein Advisory Group
PHCs	Primary Health Centres
RDA	Recommended Dietary Allowances
TCR AND TI	Tribal Cultural Research and Training Institute
TIA	Trypsin Inhibitor Activity
TIU	Trypsin Inhibitor Units
UNICEF	United Nations Children's Emergency Fund
VZM	Vizianagaram
WHO	World Health Organization.

LIST OF TABLES

LIST OF FIGURES AND ILLUSTRATIONS

FIGURES

ILLUSTRATIONS

CHAPTER 1

INTRODUCTION

Tribals constitute an important segment of the population of India, representing 7.6 per cent of the total population of the country. They are distributed in three principal territorial zones, namely, North Eastern zone, Central zone and Southern zone. They live in certain definite areas, with different dialects, cultural homogeneity, and unifying social organization. Because of the secluded living of the groups, their pattern of living, food and dietary practices and their attitudes to various aspects in general, may sometimes be different from non-tribal population. Although some work has been done on the tribal groups of India, more work is to be done to formulate appropriate programmes for improvement of the tribal communities.

Baseline information on the tribal population which includes demographic, geographic, cultural, agricultural and socio-economic characteristics is an important feature as it helps to shed some light on the constraints in the development of tribal community. Another important factor to be given much emphasis is the health status of the community. Morbidity pattern can serve as the best index of the health status. It thus helps in proper evaluation of the community health programmes and also in detection and treatment of diseases related to nutrition.

One of the major factors determining nutritional status of any community is the food consumption which is influenced by a wide range of factors like agro-climatic differences, foods grown and the availability. The dietary pattern of the aboriginal tribes of India living under various agro-climatic conditions in different isolated regions may vary widely. Studies on various tribal population of India revealed that the diets of a majority of the tribal population are nutritionally deficient (Sen Gupta, 1980; Roy and Rao, 1962; Sharma, 1979; Pratap *et al*, 1976; Rao and Satyanarayana, 1974).

Beliefs, customs and traditions influence the general pattern of living in any community (Randall and Sanjur, 1981; Cherian, 1981; Onuoha,

1982). Beliefs, inherent and integral as they are in the cultural matrix, act as invisible force in translating pre-set ideas into overt acts and customs. Handed down from generation to generation, beliefs lend authority to customs leading one to accept traditional customs and practices on their face value. The cultural pattern of each community determines the nature and extent of food behaviour found in the area. Some of the traditions followed blindly by the tribals may be good and should be preserved. Knowledge of their attitudes, traditional food and dietary practices, in general and in specific physiological conditions etc., is essential in planning appropriate nutrition and health education programmes intended for the tribals. Information of this nature in the tribal population is very limited.

It is well known that geological make up of the soil determines the occurrence of local flora, as well as cropping pattern and agricultural practices in an area. Knowledge of available food resources used by man has enabled him to survive in adverse climate. Tribals living as part of nature exploited nature to meet their food demands and some of their foods are uncommon to us. Some of their foods may be nutritionally rich and can be selectively used for bringing about nutritionally superior varieties through genetic manipulation. Therefore, nutrient evaluation of the local foods and traditional food processes adopted by the tribals provide an important tool for assessing actual nutrient contribution from their diets. Most of the dietary intake studies available were calculated with reference to general food composition tables. In spite of good deal of the work done on the nutritive value of Indian foods, similar work on the foods cultivated and consumed by Indian aboriginal population is scanty.

Food processing practices, in general, seem to differ depending on various factors like tradition, culture and individual preferences. Processing, in addition to improving the taste of the food products, add variety and diversity in food habits, and also improves nutrition. The possibility of processing of foods for preparing diverse food products is therefore essential and should be explored. The qualitative aspects of the tribal food processes help in proper planning, monitoring and evaluation of nutrition education programmes intended for tribals. The information available on the qualitative aspects of food processes adopted by triabls is limited.

The present study was carried in the two agency blocks of Viziayanagaram district, namely Bhadragiri and Pachipenta, where the tribal population is concentrated. Based on the total concentration of various tribes in the two blocks, four tribes, namely, Jatapu, Savara,

Gadaba and Kondadora, were studied. In one of the two agency blocks, namely Bhadragiri, the Indian Council of Agricultural Research has started a tribal area research project. The major objectives of the present study were to know the food and nutrient intake of women of child bearing age and pre-school children, nutrient composition of the foods cultivated and consumed by the tribals and nutrient evaluation of some of the traditional food processes, adopted by them.

CHAPTER 2

REVIEW OF LITERATURE

In the *Dictionary of Anthropology* 'Tribe' is defined as a social group usually with definite area, dialect, cultural homogeneity and unifying social organization. It may also include several subgroups. A tribe ordinarily has a leader and may have a common ancestor as well as a patron, deity. The families or small communities making up the tribe are linked through economic, religious, family or blood ties (Bhowmik *et al*, 1971). Tribals not only retained their separate ethnic and cultural identity from the non-tribal population, but each of the tribal group conserved and nurtured its distinct socio-cultural and linguistic tradition (Pratap, 1975).

The primitive tribes of India have adapted to natural environments. Their habitats differ as widely as hills, forests, plains, deserts, sea or their combination. Their economy, social institutions, beliefs and practices, and in fact their entire life-style is an adaptation to their environment and their culture can be better understood in terms of their intricately inter-related Nature-Man-Spirit-Complex (Vidyarthi, 1973-74).

FOOD AND ECONOMIC RESOURCES

Most of the tribal economy is built around agriculture either shifting or settled, agricultural and allied labour, forest resources, fishing and hunting. According to the Census from Bureau of Economics and Statistics, (1981-1982) 43.2 per cent of the Scheduled Tribes in India are cultivators and 43.7 per cent are agricultural labourers. Studies conducted on various tribes in and outside India, revealed that agriculture forms the main subsistence. A majority of the tribals attaches great importance to their land and engage in subsistence farming despite the fact that the lands are not very fertile (Onuoha, 1982).

Occupational Pattern

Based on the pattern of living, the tribals may be broadly grouped into (a) food gatherers, (b) cultivators, (c) agro-pastoral/pastoral and (d) agricultural labourers.

Food gathering forms a part of the economy with almost all the tribals. The food gathering, hunting and fishing economy of the forest tribals vary according to season cycle and area. The tribals who subsist mainly on nature for their livelihood are Todas, and some tribes of Kerala and Nilgiri hills (Roy and Ray, 1962); Onges of Andaman and Nicobar Islands (Swaminathan *et al*, 1971); Shompen tribe of Nicobar Islands (Sen Gupta, 1980); Chenchus from Andhra Pradesh (Rao and Satyanarayana, 1974; Pratap, 1973) and Kadar, a south Indian tribe (Bhowmik, 1971).

Outside India, the tribes that are reported to rely on nature for their food are the Bakitara tribe in Banyor, North West of Victoria Nyanza, Africa, and Ainus tribe of Japanese, Yezo (Sen Gupta, 1960), Iraq tribes in Arab (Al-Ani, 1980), Tasaday tribe of Philippines (Robson *et al* 1976); Amazonas of Peru (Berlin and Markell, 1977) and Alaskan tribe of Circumpolar region in Papua, New Guinea (Robson and Wadsworth, 1977).

Agro-pastoral tribes included are Akamba tribe of Nigeria (Van Steenbergen *et al*, 1984), Sandawe tribe of Central Tanzania (Newman, 1975), Tara humaras of Mexico (Cerqueira *et al*, 1979), Hansas tribe of Nigeria (Osuhor, 1980), Taswane tribe of Kalahari in Africa (Grivetti, 1979), Teso, the second largest tribe in Uganda (Biellik and Henderson, 1981), the Fulani herders of North Ferlo region in Africa (Benefice *et al*, 1984) and Bakitara tribe of Victoria Nyanza in Africa (Sen Gupta, 1960).

Agricultural labour and the related work in various plantations and forest departments form the basis of economy of the greater number of tribes. Whenever possible, the tribal people supplement their income by raising poultry, weaving, and gathering various forest products (Roy and Rao, 1962; Sen Gupta, 1980).

The pattern of agriculture varies from one tribe to another depending partly upon the opportunities and partly upon the traditions of the people (Burling, 1965). A large part of the tribal cultivation is hill or shifting cultivation and whenever possible a nearby water source is exploited to induce artificial irrigation. This is called 'Terrace' cultivation followed mainly in cultivating rice. The tribals who live on plains or lower regions of hills practice settled, and also wet cultivation depending on the irrigation sources available. (Bhowmik, 1971). Among the Indian tribes, Tripura tribes (Rao, 1971), Koyas and Maria Gonds of Central India (Pingale,

1973), tribes of NEFA, Gonds and Murias of Madhya Pradesh, Santal tribes of Bihar (Sen Gupta, 1980) are reported to practice both shifting and settled agriculture.

Some tribes outside India also practice hill or 'slash and burn' agriculture (Horner *et al*, 1981). A minor flood-agriculture is reported to be practiced by Cocopah Indian tribes in Colorado (Calloway and Gibbs, 1976). Among the tribes who practiced subsistence agriculture are Igbo tribes in the South Eastern Part of Nigeria (Onuoha, 1982), Solomon Community of South Pacific Islands (Joseph, 1981), Kikuyu tribe of Kenya (Hoorweg and Niemeyer, 1980), Hopi tribe of North East Arizona (Kuhnlein and Calloway, 1977), the Aguaruna tribe in Peru (Robson and Wadsworth, 1977), Shaamba tribe of Tanzania (Fleuret, 1979), and Miskito Indians of North Eastern Nicaragua (Horner *et al*, 1977).

Industrialization and development of commercial centres, communication systems and provision of opportunities for crop and animal husbandry are reported to have brought some changes in the occupation and food habits, traditional cooking practices, food gathering and agricultural practices of tribals (Robson and Wadsworth, 1977; Kuhnlein and Calloway, 1977; Calloway and Gibbs, 1976; Horner *et al* 1981; Joseph, 1981; Fleuret, 1979; Swaminathan *et al*, 1971; Newman, 1975)

MORBIDITY

Morbidity can be described in terms of the incidence and prevalence of certain diseases or disabilities. It is usually expressed as a rate: The number of cases of diseases per 1000 persons at risk. The most accurate way of assessing morbidity rate is through epidemiological survey. However, reporting cases through health systems, surveillance also does provide some indication of the relevant magnitude of the disease incidence as well as the trends in control and prevention (WHO, 1981).

Morbidity in Indian tribes

Various studies on health status of the Indian tribals indicated that the prevalence of disease varies with the location, season, literacy, income levels and various other factors. The incidence of angular stomatitis, glossitis, night blindness, photophobia, malnutrition and non-nutritional disorders like scabies, dental caries and malaria too are found to be high in the tribes of Andhra Pradesh and Central India (NIN, 1973; Pratap *et al*, 1976; Pingale, 1973).

Sharma (1971) evaluated the health status of Konds of Orissa and reported the incidence of gastric disorders, (19.58 per cent), throat/ respiratory infection (18.36 per cent), skin diseases (10.99 per cent), malaria (10.81 per cent), muscular pains and avitaminosis (3.69 per cent) and anaemia (2.31 per cent) in the tribals.

Ali (1978-79) in his study on Kutia Konds of Orissa, reported high incidence of diarrhoea, dysentery, helminthic worm infections, malaria, and typhoid, and a genetic disease, sickle-cell anaemia was also reported to be present in the tribes.

A study on tribal of Abor hills of Assam State indicated that the incidence of goitre in two areas of Padam and Minyoung is 13.1% and 9.8% respectively (Sen Gupta, 1960). A study on Monpas tribe of NEFA reported an incidence of goitre (3.6 per cent), angular stomatitis (8 per cent) in the tribals (NIN, 1967).

In Onge tribe of Andaman and Nicobar Islands, fungal infection of the skin is the most common disease. Moderate degree of eosinophilia is also reported. However, the incidence of anaemia, malaria are said to be rare among these tribals (NIN, 1969).

A general health survey of nearly 4000 tribals of Madhya Pradesh revealed that only 23 per cent of the population are in good health and 33 per cent are in poor health. Malaria is found to be common in the tribals. Incidence of dental caries (17 per cent), anaemia (11 per cent), vitamin deficiencies (5 per cent) is reported in the tribals of Madhya Pradesh (Gore *et al*, 1977)

A health study on tribals of East Godavari district showed that respiratory infection, fever and gastroenteritis and various aches and pains are common in these tribals and among the nutritional deficiencies, 0.9 per cent has night blindness and 9.7 per cent anaemia (Pushpamma *et al*, 1983).

Various studies in India indicated that unhygienic living conditions of the tribals are the major cause of skin infection and gastric disorders (Ali, 1978-79; NIN, 1973; Pingale, 1973)

Morbidity in tribals Abroad

A clinical health study on Amazonas of Peru indicated that certain parasitic infections mainly hookworm, whipworm and ascariasis are prevalent in the community. Anaemia, dental caries and inflammatory diseases of gums are also said to be common in the tribals (Berlin and Markell, 1977)

Calloway and Gibbs (1976) in their study on Cocopah (a small Colorado Indian tribe) reported that the major chronic diseases of the Cocopah are alcoholism and diabetes. Also, a high incidence of liver, kidney and gallbladder diseases, gastroenteritis, colitis and endemic cases of tuberculosis and rabies are reported to be common in the community.

FOOD CONSUMPTION PRACTICES

Staples

The staples include cereals, starchy fruits, roots and tubers depending on the seasonal availability . Various scientists in the past reported that rice, wheat, corn, sorghum, bajra, ragi and minor millets are the staple foods of the tribals in India and abroad (Pingale, 1973; Bhattacharya, *et al*, 1972; Sen Gupta, 1980; Gore et al, 1977; Pratap et al, 1976; Gopaladas et al, 1983; Roy and Rao, 1962; Rao and Satyanarayana, 1974; Osuhor, 1980; Fleuret, 1979; Greenhouse, 1981; Newman, 1975; Kuhnlein and Calloway, 1977; Benefice *et al*, 1984; Van Steenbergen *et al*, 1984; Cerqueira et al, 1979; Al-Ani, 1980). A kind of cereal namely Annayat (*Coix lachryam*) is reported to be consumed by Abors living on higher regions of hills (Sen Gupta, 1980).

Pulses

Pulses are said to form only a minor food item of most of the tribes in India. (Gore, *et al*, 1977; Rao and Satyanarayana, 1974). However, pulses like horsegram, redgram and, to a lesser extent greengram, are reported to be consumed in considerable quantities by some tribals. (Sharma, 1971; Sen Gupta, 1980; Roy and Rao, 1962; NIN, 1973)

Studies on tribals living abroad revealed that a variety of pulses enriched their dietaries and pulses like chickpea, tepary beans, kidney bean, peas (*Pisum sativum*:) bonavist bean (*Lablab niger*), pigeon pea, lima bean and mung bean are said to be cultivated and consumed by tribes of Africa and America (Biellik and Henderson, 1981; Newman, 1975; Cerqueira *et al*, 1979; Kuhnlein and Calloway 1977; Calloway and Gibbs, 1976; Hoorweg and Niemeyer, 1980; Van Steenbergen, *et al*, 1984).

Roots and Tubers

Roots and tuber consumption is reported to be seasonal and their quantitative share in the tribal dietaries is reported to be small (Gore *et al*, 1977). However, tapioca, yam (*Dioscorea sp.*), and potatoes are reported to form the staple food of Malapandaramas and Kanikkars of Kerala and certain tribes of Nilgiri hills (Sen Gupta, 1980; Roy and Rao, 1962). The roots *theetheknow gege* (botanical name not known) are reported to be staple food of Onge tribe of Andaman and Nicobar Islands (Swaminathan *et al*, 1971)

Studies conducted on tribals outside India revealed that potato, sweet potato, cassava, yam, cocoyam, arrow root, and faro, form the staple food of the majority (Joseph, 1981; Onuoha, 1982; Fleuret, 1979; Biellik and Henderson, 1981; Robson *et al*, 1976; Van Steenbergen, *et al*, 1984; Kuhnlein and Calloway, 1977; Berlin and Markell, 1977; Hoorweg and Niemeyer, 1976; Newman, 1975; Horner *et al*, 1981)

Vegetables

Vegetable production is reported to be a part of the tribal living (Sen Gupta, 1980). Vegetables supplement many of the tribal diets, and quite often tribal diet consists of cooked rice or millets and some boiled vegetables like brinjals, beans, gourds, pumpkin, onion, green chillies, mushrooms etc. (Roy and Rao, 1962; Rao, 1971). Green leafy vegetables either cultivated or collected from jungles, fields or from the stream beds are reported to be consumed by the tribals of India. Some tribes are reported to have a special liking for greens and consume greens in larger quantities (Pingale, 1973; Sen Gupta, 1980, Bhowmik, 1971; Sharma, 1979). However, vegetable consumption is reported to be not common with the Onge tribe of Andaman and Nicobar Islands (Rao, 1971; Swaminathan et al, 1971)

Vegetables like mushrooms, tomatoes, and green plantains are reported to be consumed in very limited quantities by various tribals (Newman, 1975; Hoorweg and Niemeyer, 1980; Robson and Wadsworth, 1977; Horner *et al*, 1981). However, leafy vegetables also form an important item in the tribal dietaries outside India. Enormous varieties of green leaves like tulip leaves, sweet potato leaves and leaves of cassava, amaranth, cowpea, pumpkin, cabbage, kele, swamp feru and bamboo shoots of various kinds are reported to be consumed by them (Robson and

Wadsworth, 1977; Newman, 1975; Joseph, 1981; Hoorweg and Niemeyer, 1980; Fleuret, 1979)

Non-vegetarian Foods

Meat is greatly appreciated by a majority of the tribes and are reported to be particularly not fastidious about selecting animals for meat, with few exceptions like Todas, a pastoral tribe. Domestic animals as well as wild life go into their dietaries as and when available. In many areas, pigs and fowls are reported to be reared and pork is said to be the most favourite item (Rao, 1971). Meat of a type of Yak (*Bos frontalis*) and 'ESSO' a semi-domesticated animal is reported to be a prized food for Abors (Rao, 1971). Sacrificing of animals like buffaloes, cow, bull, pig, fowl etc., on special occasions and sharing the flesh among the villagers is said to be common with the tribals. (Roy and Rao, 1962;, Sen Gupta, 1980). Various insects and succulent larvae of certain insects are reported to be consumed by the tribals (Roy and Rao, 1962; Grivetti, 1979; Sen Gupta, 1980). In spite of the emphatic account of various kinds of flesh foods, consumption of it by the tribals is reported to be low. The tribals are too poor to kill their domestic animals very often and wild animals too are not always available, (Roy and Rao, 1962). However, pork consumption by tribals of Andaman and Nicobar Islands is reported to be as high as 2 ½ kg per day per head (Rao, 1971). Octopus, shark, prawns, sea turtles, varieties of fishes, shrimps, lobsters, cress, etc., are reported to be mostly consumed by Onges of Andaman (Sen Gupta, 1980; Swaminathan *et al*, 1971). Fish, are liked by most of the tribes, but only few tribes can afford to get it regularly. (Rao, 1971). However, dried fish is reported to be used by various tribals in small quantities as a flavouring agent in vegetable preparations (Roy and Rao, 1962). Eggs are generally not consumed by the tribals and are mainly used for hatching (Gore *et al*, 1977). However, hen eggs and turtle eggs are reported to be consumed by Chenchus of Andhra Pradesh, and Onges of Nicobar Islands (Rao, 1971; Sen Gupta, 1980)

Some of the studies on tribals, carried out abroad show that various kinds of birds, insects, reptiles form a part of their daily diet. Hunted wert hog, bear, spring hare, monkey giraffe, hyena, leopard, monitor lizard, lark, francolin gerbil, cattle, pig, goat, chicken, hare, sheep, bandicoots, lizards, geese, jungle fowl, snakes, ducks, bats, frogs are reported to be consumed by most of the tribes (WeiWo and Draper, 1975; Berlin and Markell, 1977; Hoorweg and Niemeyer, 1980; Newman,

1975; Al-Ani, 1980; Benefice *et al*, 1984; Osuhor, 1980; Kuhnlein and Calloway, 1977). Marine source like various kinds of fish, turtle, water snakes etc., whale, seal, carbou, walrus are reported to be consumed by tribes of Circumpolar region (Robson and Wadsworth, 1977; Joseph, 1981)

Milk and Milk Products

Milk is a rare food item in tribal dietaries and milch cattle are reared for agriculture and meat purposes and not for milking (Gore *et al*, 1977). However, Todas are reported to consume good amounts of butter, buttermilk and curd though milk as such is rarely consumed (Rao, 1971), and this may be because they are the buffalo herdsmen. Milk products, cheese and butter obtained from cow and yak are reported to be consumed by Monpas of NEFA (Sen Gupta, 1980).

Studies carried out abroad revealed that the pastoral tribes mainly subsist on milk and milk products. (Hoorweg and Niemeyer, 1980; Newman, 1975; Benefice *et al*, 1984; Sen Gupta, 1960). Iraq tribes of Arab are reported to consume camel milk (Al-Ani, 1980). Tribes from Nigeria and Mexico also are reported to consume milk (Van Steenbergen, *et al*, 1984; Osuhor, 1980; Cerqueira et al, 1979; Grivetti, 1979). However, milk is not reported to be a traditional item with the tribes of Colorado and Pacific Islands (Calloway and Gibbs, 1976; Joseph, 1981)

Nuts and Oilseeds

Nuts and oilseeds like sesame, castor and groundnut are reported to form the major cash crops of various tribes in and outside India (Rao and Satyanarayana, 1974; Sen Gupta, 1980; Pingale, 1973; Biellik and Henderson, 1981; Berlin and Markell, 1977; Newman, 1975; Robson and Wadsworth, 1977; Hoorweg and Niemeyer, 1980)

Fats and Oils

Fats and oils do not form a usual item in most of the tribal dietaries. However, butter made from the milk of cow, yak and sheep milk, pork fat, oils extracted from mustard, sesame, groundnut and Mohua seeds are reported to be used in small quantities by some tribals (Pingale, 1973; Sen Gupta, 1960; Sen Gupta, 1980; Rao, 1971, Al-Ani, 1980; Joseph, 1981)

Fruits

Fruits mostly collected from forests and a few cultivated ones like papaya, plantain, jackfruit, are reported to be consumed by many tribals. Pandanus (screw pine), and a special kind of fruit mangrove are consumed by Onges of Andaman and Nicobar Islands. Various fruits like papaya, jackfruit, pandanus, custard apple, citrus fruits, figs, grapes, bread fruit, and squashes etc., and many other wild fruits are reported to be consumed by the tribes in India and abroad. (Swaminathan *et al* 1971; Berlin and Markell, 1977; Hoorweg and Niemeyer, 1980; Horner, *et al*, 1981; Calloway and Gibbs, 1976; Joseph, 1981; Robson and Wadsworth, 1977; Benefice *et al*, 1984; Robson *et al*, 1976; Newman, 1975). Iraq tribes of Arab, however, are reported to take no fruits except dates (Al-Ani, 1980). A strange practice of ripening fruits to a pleasant tart taste by burying under piles of moist, warm cattle dung, is reported to be practiced by Tswane tribe of Africa (Grivetti 1979)

Sugar and Jaggery

Sugar and molasses are reported to be rarely consumed by the tribals. However, honey collected from woods, is reported to be a common article of food for most of the tribals. (Rao, 1971; Swaminathan *et al*, 1971; Sharma; 1979; Berlin and Markell, 1977; Newman, 1975).

Spices and Condiments

The use of spices and condiments by the tribals is negligible and the most commonly used ones are chillies, turmeric and salt. Monpas tribe prepare a special masala like chvrpin from a bean 'lebi' to be used in every side dish (Rao, 1971). Curry powder, ginger powder and salt are reported to be used by African tribes (Hoorweg and Niemeyer, 1980).

Unusual foods

Unusual foods available in the forest during the monsoon period form the staple food for most of the tribals specially to those living in hilly areas. The yield of agricultural produce being poor, tribals have to depend on the forest produce during the lean period. Various unusual foods like roots of various *Dioscorea* species, wild mushrooms, bamboo shoots, wild mangoes and its stones, red ants, wild millets, wild rice which grows near paddy fields, a kind of leguminous seed *Mucuna pruriens* and *Caryota* palm pith etc., are reported to be consumed by the tribals of India (Pingale, 1973; Pratap *et al*, 1976; Sen Gupta, 1980; Ali 1978-79).

Waterlilies, nuts and seeds of tamarind, cycad, pandanus (screw pine), shoots of fan palm and Kentia palm, bamboo shoots, *seeds* of *pinus edulis*, seeds of *Boscia senegalensin*, young leaf, shoots and leaf buds of palms of Caryota, seeds of baobab (*Adansonia digitato*), mongongonut (*Ricino dendron rautanenii schinz*), tsin bean (*Bauhinia esculenta* and B. Macrantha), sago palm grubs, bark, root, resins, leaf, nuts of some fruit species, are reported to be consumed by various tribes outside India (Robson and Wadsworth, 1977; Kuhnlein and Calloway, 1977; Robson *et al*, 1976; Benefice *et al*, 1984; Newman, 1975; Lee, 1973). During famine period, wild roots of *Caropegia* spp. (*Thylachium africanum*) are boiled and eaten whereas the roots *Panicum heterostachyum* are reported to be eaten raw and seeds of *Dactyloctenium giganteum* and leaves of *Coccinia trilobata* are boiled and eaten (Newman, 1975).

Beverages

Alcoholic beverages are generally consumed by tribals. Seasonality and availability of foods, determine the source of food in the preparation of alcoholic beverages. Barring some tribes of Kerala and Nilgiri, the tribals are generally habituated to alcoholic drinks. Alcohol plays a significant role in the social and religious life of some tribes (Rao, 1971). Cereal and millet based liquors consumed by the tribals are said to be homebrewed undistilled liquors. The millet-based less alcoholic beverages are said to be nutritious providing protein, minerals and vitamins (Sen Gupta, 1962). Padam Abors prepare '*Apong*' an alcoholic beverage with ragi. Baigas, Murias and some other tribes of Madhya Pradesh are also reported to prepare a millet based alcoholic beverage. To the cooked millet, a fermented mixture 'Ara' is said to be added which acts as an intoxicating agent. An alcoholic beverage '*bang chang*' is reported to be prepared by Monpas with ground cereal or millet (Rao, 1971; Roy and Rao, 1962). Rice is said to be used in alcohol preparation by Gallong Abors (Roy and Rao, 1962). Liquor prepared from fermented mango juice is reported to be taken by tribals of Srikakulam district (Pratap *et al*, 1976). Mahua flowers, are said to be the basic ingredient in the preparation of liquors (Sharma, 1979; Roy, 1976; Pingale, 1973; Daspatnaik, 1976; Roy and Rao, 1962; NIN, 1973; Rao and Satyanarayana, 1974; TCR and TI Hyderabad, 1969). One to two litres of the alcohol per individual is reported to be consumed by the tribals of Srikakulam district, and this provides about one third of their calorie intake (Pratap *et al*, 1976).

Interesting facts have come to light about tribes outside India in the preparation of home-made alcoholic beverages. Amazonas of Peru use cassava (*Manihot esculenta*) in the preparation of beer namely '*nijamash*' a substance about the consistency of buttermilk. The beer is said to be prepared by boiling manioc roots, and mashing the soft cooked roots with a long, flattened stick. Large mouthfuls of the soft roots are masticated until liquid comes out and then spat back into the same pot which is allowed to ferment. (Berlin and Markell, 1977). The source for preparation of beverages seems to vary depending on the season and availability of foods. Tender leaves of wild species are sought for brewing various berries, fruits, and a few succulent bulbs. The juice thus extracted is consumed either fresh or after fermentation or blended with milk. In winter, the decoction obtained by boiling the ground, roasted roots of *Boscia albitrunca* and *Grewia flava* are served as a substitute of coffee by some African tribes. (Grivetti, 1979). A favourite drink of Fulani herdsmen is said to be a milk beverage which is prepared by souring milk in the shade. Another sweetened beverage, chian green tea is also reported to be relished by them (Benefice *et al*, 1984). Red sorghum or ragi is said to form the basic ingredient in preparing an alcoholic beverage by Tanzania tribes (Newman, 1975). Tribes of South Pacific Islands are reported to consume coconut toddy obtained after fermentation of young coconut shoots (Joseph, 1981).

FOOD STORAGE PRACTICES OF TRIBALS

The habit of storing excess food is more evident in the tribes living in the dense forests where more surplus can be collected. However, since their food pattern is related to cycle of seasons, food storage practices among the tribals appear to be not popular. A variety of wild foods like wild tubers and flowers of *Bassia latiofolia*, mushroom, bamboo shoots, stones of wild mango, red ants, wild leafy vegetables, green leaves and flowers of *Hibiscus subdariffa* and pith of caryota palm and meat are reported to be stored by sundrying (Rao, 1971; Swaminathan *et al*, 1971; Pingale, 1973; Sen Gupta, 1980; Roy and Rao, 1962; Bhowmik, 1971; Pratap *et al*, 1976; Pratap, 1973).

Some of the storage practices of tribes outside India are storage of meat, fish and turtle by smoking or sundrying or cooking till half done in salted water and sundrying; storing cooked caryota palm pith by wrapping in leaf; storing of wild leaves, bark, resins, fruits of some plants, roots and yoghurt by sundrying; soaking dates in small amounts of water and storing in the bags made of sheep or goat skin (Grivetti, 1979; Robson *et al*, 1976; Newman, 1975; Al-Ani, 1980; Horner *et al*, 1981; Weiwo and Draper, 1975).

DIETARY PATTERN OF TRIBALS

Generally, three meals a day is a common practice with the tribals. The morning meal consists of cooked cereal kept overnight with or without *conjee*. The noon meal consists of millet gruel (Porridge) prepared from fermented ragi or other unfermented millets. In the evening, freshly prepared hot rice with vegetable curry and/or dhal is reported to be the usual meal pattern with various tribals (Bhowmik, 1971; Pratap *et al*, 1976; Pingale; 1973; Pratap, 1973; Sen Gupta, 1980). Onges of Andaman and Nicobar have three or four meals a day. Pork and fish are reported to be taken with all the meals in combination with roots, tubers and honey depending on the availability (Swaminathan, *et al*, 1971).

The dietary studies on the tribals outside India, also revealed that the usual meal pattern of most of the tribes is three meals a day and consumption of left over rice of previous night in the morning is common (Kuhnlein and Calloway, 1977; Al-Ani, 1980; Hoorweg and Niemeyer, 1980; Robson and Wadsworth 1977); Van Steenbergen *et al*, 1984; Benefice *et al*, 1984; Fleuret, 1979). However, some tribals are reported to be satisfied with two meals a day (Newman, 1975; Robson *et al*, 1976; Calloway and Gibbs, 1976). Australian aboriginals have no fixed meal pattern (Robson and Wadsworth, 1977). However, the meal pattern of Iraq nomadic tribes of Arab is reported to be wheat in combination with camel milk/ date syrup/yoghurt/ghee, and the diet was same all round the year (Al-Ani, 1980).

Cooking Practices

Cooking practices of the tribals are said to be unique. Tribes of Madhya Pradesh prepare a beverage known as 'Pej' by boiling cereal with buttermilk for a long time. Abors of NEFA do not wash cereal/millets before cooking, nor drain the water after cooking (Rao, 1971). Cooking of rice/millets/ pulse with mahua flowers is practised by Bhils and Gonds of Madhya

Pradesh and Gonds of Andhra Pradesh (Bhomik, 1971; Rao and Satyanarayana, 1974). Cooking of rice in buttermilk instead of water is reported to be practised by Toda herdsmen when milk supply is abundant (Roy and Rao, 1962; Rao, 1971). Adding sour buttermilk to millet gruel and leaving it in shade to be kneaded and steamed for consumption is practised by Furlo tribe. A kind of leaf (*Baolab leaves*) (*Adansonia digitata*) powder is added to the gruel to give it a semolina like consistency (Benefice *et al*, 1984). A maize porridge of stiff, heavy, and stodgy consistency is preferred by tribes of Tanzania (Fleuret, 1979). A tradition of adding vegetables, potatoes, green bananas to the cereal preparation is also reported (Hoorweg and Niemeyer, 1980; Newman, 1975). Pima Indians of Arizona are reported to prepare hidden ash bread called '*hyashpmatai chimait*' by pouring a smooth batter made from wheat flour, into the depression of hot ashes (obtained by burning a particular wood). It is then covered with the ash, topped with a few live coals and allowed to bake for approximately an hour. The bread prepared in this manner is reported to contain five times as much iron and 4 times as much calcium than the original batter (Greenhouse, 1981). Caryota starch is prepared by pounding caryota palm pith and the powder dissolved in water and decanted into troughs and allowed to precipitate which is cooked and consumed by Tasaday tribe of Philippines (Robson *et al*, 1976).

Cooking meat and greens together is reported to be practised by Abors (Sen Gupta, 1960). Onges of Andaman and Nicobar Islands have a peculiar habit of cooking pork meat. It is wrapped between leaves and then boiled or roasted on red hot stones placed in a hole. The hole then is made airtight by mud plastering and opened after 3 or 4 hours. The pork thus cooked is consumed without seasoning by salt or spices. Pig fat is reported to be extracted by prolonged cooking of pork which is used as a subsidiary dish by the Onges (Swaminathan *et al*, 1971). Fatty little insect larvae, is reported to be consumed by Indian tribals after seasoning with chillies and salt (Roy and Rao, 1962; Grivetti, 1979; Sen Gupta, 1980).

Baking, roasting or steaming of meat, fish, roots, banana *etc*., by wrapping in leaves and placing them on live coal or pre-heated stones or on direct fire is practised by various tribals outside India (Berlin and Markell, 1977; Robson *et al*, 1970; Joseph, 1981). Cocopah Indians of native American group are said to consume meat and eggs after frying (Calloway and Gibbs, 1976). Onges of Andaman and Nicobar Islands boil pandanus (screw pine) leaves and consume the supernatant (Swaminathan *et al*, 1971). A tribe in south Pacific Islands is reported to cook greens with coconut milk (Joseph, 1981).

ATTITUDES AND BELIEFS ABOUT FOOD

General Food Taboos

Superstitions and beliefs invariably influence the attitudes towards foods. Food habits and beliefs differ among the different tribes and even among the communities within the tribes. Certain foods are prohibited from consumption by all, and in some cases, the food restrictions are determined by age, sex and physiological status and seasonal availability (Onuoha, 1982).

The Indian diet, especially in the rural or tribal setting, is greatly influenced by the two established systems of medicine—Ayurvedic and Unani, both of which classify foods as hot or cold, according to the effect they are believed to create on body mechanisms (Gopaldas *et al*, 1983). Prohibition from consumption of beef, meat, fish, tiger, panther, snake, frog, hawk, vulture, dog, cow, cat, horse, bear, are widely prevalent in various tribes (Rao, and Satyanarayana, 1974; NIN, 1967 and 1973; Sen Gupta, 1960; Bhowmik, 1971).

Food fads and fallacies of the tribes of Iraq are worth mentioning. The flesh of bush pig (*Potamo choerus*) and other mammals which are thought to resemble swine, hedge hog (*Erinacaus frontalis*), hyrax (*Procavia capensis*) porcupine (*Hystrix africaeaustrelis*), wolf, black backed jackal (*Canis mesomelas arenarum*), cape fox (*Vulpes chama*), spotted hyena (*Croculauocuta*), rodents are prohibited for adults. However, these are not prohibited for children. Children are prohibited from eating wild fowl, birds' eggs, red crested korhaan, guinea fowl, *etc*. Frogs are reported to be a taboo for Tloskwe community but not for other communities. Fish of all kinds are relished by one community but prohibited by other communities of the same locality. Uncooked liver is believed to be good for health and vitality. Children are not given eggs with the fear that they may develop sweet teeth which would lead them to steal when they grow up. Sacrificing and consumption of local cows and buffaloes is prohibited as it is believed that they are incarnation of the ancestors. Antelopes and pigs are prohibited as animal food, the latter for their dirty habits. Consumption of three leafed yam is prohibited as it is said to cause misfortune. Camel milk and dates are believed to be good for health and longevity. Right side of hyena is prohibited from consumption but left side is allowed for consumption (Al-Ani, 1980)

Infant feeding practices

Information available with regard to infant feeding practices of the tribals is scanty. Feeding of colostrum to infants is practiced in the tribals of Gujarat, East Godavari district and Madhya Pradesh (Gopaldas *et al*, 1983; Pushpamma *et al*, 1983; NIN, 1983; Subha Rani, 1984). The Onges of Andaman and Nicobar Islands also breast feed their children on the first two days after the delivery (Swaminathan *et al*, 1971). Breast feeding is reported to be continued till 12 to 36 months by various tribals (Pratap *et al*, 1976; Rao and Satyanarayana 1974, Battacharya *et al*, 1972; Al-Ani, 1980; Gore *et al*, 1977; Pushpamma *et al* 1971; Osuhor, 1980; Robson and Wadsworth, 1977; Hoorweg and Niemeyer, 1980). Tribals of East Godavari district are said to believe that as long as the children are on breast milk there is no need for supplementary foods (Pushpamma *et al*, 1983).

Though tribals wean their infants before one year, breast milk is reported to be continued for two to three years (Osuhor *et al*, 1980; Horner *et al*, 1977; Pratap *et al*, 1976; NIN, 1979, 1982 and 1983:, Hoorweg and Niemeyer, 1980; Robson and Wadsworth, 1977). Onges start weaning by the second month though breast feeding is said to continue till two years. In Onge tribe, the children are adapted to adult diet by eight to nine months (Swaminathan *et al*, 1971). Weaning foods of various tribals are reported to be varied like maize gruel, buffalo/cow milk, cereal/millet flour porridge, mashed banana, mashed potato, sweet potato, *chapati* soaked in milk or dhal soup, mashed vegetables, bread, mohua alcohol, soft cooked rice, coffee and oat meal (Osuhor, 1980; Battacharya *et al*, 1972; Hoorweg and Niemeyer, 1980; Van Steenbergen *et al*, 1984; Gopaldas *et al*, 1983; Horner *et al*, 1981). Some of the tribals abroad feed their infants with honey, turtle eggs, flesh portions of small fish, or roots (Robson and Wadsworth, 1977).

Food taboos related to pregnancy and lactation

Women of child bearing age are prohibited from eating eggs. The pregnant women are prohibited from consuming pork due to a belief that children born might get spotted skins. Snails are prohibited for pregnant women with the fear that children would be afflicted with excessive saliva (Onuoha, 1982). Special diet for pregnant and lactating women is thought to be not necessary by some Indian tribals (Gore *et al*, 1977).

Some of the food fads and fallacies of Gujarat tribes reported are as follows. *Mahuva* alcohol (*Mahuva indica*) given during and after delivery is believed to combat tiredness, staunch postpartum bleeding, and said to cleanse the woman's gastrointestinal tract. Some tribal women believe that consumption of alcohol by the women causes diarrhoea in infants. During lactation, bajra, redgram, and a special drink *Sua-ka-pani* made from the bark of a tree-Sindha (*Viethenia somnifera*) is believed to immunise the child from all possible diseases. Consumption of salt, chillies, wheat, blackgram dhal, jowar, new maize and moth beans is believed to make the breast milk indigestible to the child. For a pregnant woman, jaggery, black pepper and wheat are considered good, whereas, consumption of salt, chillies, blackgram, maize, jowar, ghee, moth beans, groundnut, curd, coconut milk and new rice, are considered to be injurious to the foetus (Gopaldas *et al*, 1983).

Gege, a tuber is preferred for lactating women by Onge tribes as it is believed to augment milk production (Swaminathan *et al*, 1971). Coconut, bajra, jaggery, ghee and earth worms are considered to be effective galactogogues by some tribes in Gujarat (Gopaldas *et al*, 1983). The tribes of Madhya Pradesh consider a tuber '*Ban Mura*', redgram dhal, jaggery and ghee galactogogues (NIN, 1983).

Taboos related to health and illness

During diarrhoea and illness Onge tribe prefer to eat carbohydrate rich foods like Teethekotu roots but avoid foods rich in fat, like pork (Swaminathan *et al*, 1971). Tribes of Srikakulam district believe that rice beer has curative properties and cooling effect on the body (Pratap *et al*, 1976). Jowar, blackgram, peanuts, a wild fruit (*Zizyphus mauritiana*) and banana are believed to cause flatulence. Brinjal, flaked rice, millet, cluster beans, potato, pumpkin, papaya, onion and sugar are considered hot foods whereas redgram, banana curd, and rice are thought to be cold foods and believed to be eaten in the contrasting seasons (Gopaldas *et al*, 1983). Honey is prohibited for children considering it 'hot' food and is also believed to lead to forgetfulness in children (Grivetti, 1979). Maria Gonds of Bastar district of Madhya Pradesh consider that rice gruel kept overnight with or without curd keep the stomach cool. Blackgram and brinjal are believed to cause constipation. A herbal medicine of the bark of a mango tree ground with water and taken with sugar is believed to be effective in diarrhoea (NIN, 1983).

FOOD AND NUTRIENT INTAKE

Studies on the food and nutrient intake of the tribal women of child bearing age are limited. However, those few available on the food intake of the tribals in general, will be of some help in analysing their nutrient gaps.

Food and nutrient intake of tribes in India

Pingale (1973) reported an intake of 430 g and 767 g of staple grains by Koya and Maria Gonds of Central India, respectively. The diets of Koyas are reported to be mainly millet based, as millets form 70 per cent in the diets of Koyas and 18 per cent in Maria Gonds and the remaining is said to be contributed from rice. The reported mean nutrient intake of Maria Gonds and Koya tribes is given in Table 2.1.

TABLE 2.1
Per capita nutrient intake of Maria Gonds and Koyas of Central India

Nutrients	*Maria Gonds*		*Koyas*	
Energy (Kcal)	2958	± 326	1824	± 402
Protein (g)	73.92	± 8.15	61.08	± 15.85
Calcium (mg)	317.89	± 52.14	595.88	± 126.65
Iron (mg)	33.85	± 3.61	26.02	± 6.82
β-Carotene (μg)	613.51	± 27.83	602.51	± 126.89
Vitamin C (mg)	23.63	± 8.47	24.32	± 4.79
Thiamine (mg)	1.273	± 0.23	1.69	± 0.47
Riboflavin (mg)	0.944	± 0.13	0.70	± 0.15

The mean food and nutrient intake of 31 tribes in four regions of India as reported by Sen Gupta (1980) is given in Table 2.2

TABLE 2.2

Mean food intake of 31 tribes in four regions of India

Foods (g)	*NEFA*	*Eastern India*	*Central India*	*Southern India*
Staple grain	622	660	584	278
Roots and Tubers	53	31	-	492
Vegetables/Fruits	51	85	120	103
Flesh foods	11	Neg	Neg	Neg
Pulses	-	30	34	8
Milk and milk products	-	14	23	108
Oils/Fats	-	-	-	9

Sharma (1979) in his study on Koyas of Orissa reported an intake of cereal to be 475 g, pulses 30 g and fruits 30 g. The consumption of wild green leafy vegetables is reported to be high among these tribes. The average nutrient intake of an adult Kond is said to contain energy 1708 Kcal, protein 43 g, calcium 1.2 g and iron 62.7 mgs. In tribes of Orissa the per capita intake of Energy is 1665 Kcal and protein 36 g (Gore *et al*, 1977). Sharma (1979) reported a Calorie intake of 1385 Kcal and protein 45 g in some tribes of Orissa.

The tribals of East Godavari district reported to consume per day 572 g cereals, 51 g other vegetables, 19 g roots and tubers, 13 g flesh foods, 279 ml milk and milk products, 44 g condiments and spices. Consumption of pulses, green leafy vegetables, fruits, oils, sugar and jaggery is reported to be negligible. The mean nutrient intake is reported to be Calories 2206 Kcal, Protein 54 g, β-carotene 344 μg, thiamine 0.82 mg, riboflavin 0.78 mg, niacin 15 mg, vitamin C 21 mg, calcium 418 mg, iron 25 mg (Pushpamma *et al*, 1983).

Pratap *et al* (1976) reported the food intake of pregnant and lactating women of Andhra Pradesh and the values given by them are presented in Table 2.3.

TABLE 2.3

Mean food intake of pregnant and lactating tribal women of Srikakulam district, Andhra Pradesh

Foods (g)	*Pregnant women*	*Lactating women*
Cereals	372	426
Pulses	75	78
Leafy vegetables	60	56
Vegetables	33	68
Flesh foods	12	13
Milk and Milk products	17	24

There are very few studies available on the seasonal variation in food intake of the tribals are reported. The food intake of Chenchu tribes of Andhra Pradesh in summer and rainy seasons are reported as cereals 565 g and 388 g; pulses 82 g and nil in rainy season, flesh foods 44 g and 12 g, leafy vegetables 89 g and 24 g, roots and tubers 81 g and 36 g, respectively. In rainy season the intake of milk and milk products and fruits reported to be 74 g and 30 g, respectively and nil consumption in summer. Consumption of other vegetables, sugar and jaggery is reported to be negligible in both the seasons. The intake of nutrients reported in summer and rainy season is energy 1691 Kcal and 2705 Kcal, protein 81 g and 45 g, β—carotene 911 μg and 131 μg, calcium 800 mg and 860 mg, iron 58 mg and 37 mg. respectively (Pratab, 1973).

The reported nutrient intake of the tribals of Gujarat (Gopaldas *et al*, 1983), Kenya (Van Steenbergen *et al*, 1979) are given in Table 2.4.

TABLE 2.4

Mean nutrient intake of tribal women in Gujarat, Kenya and Mexico

Nutrients	*Gujarat*[1] *(13-19yr)*	*Kenya*[2] *(13-18 r)*	*Mexico*[3] *(18-70 yr)*
Calories (kcal)	2244 ± 28	1796	2552 ± 342
Protein (g)	81 ± 1.5	59	79 ± 11
Calcium(mg)	536 ± 2	395	650 ± 103
Iron (mg)	27 ± 0.8	19	25 ± 3
β-carotene μg	764 ± 43	303	—
Vitamin C (mg)	28 ± 5.2	68	84 ± 26
Thiamine (mg)	NA	1.9	1.9 ± 0.2
Riboflavin (mg)	NA	0.8	1.1 ± 0.2
Niacin (mg)	NA	68	13.7 ± 2.0

1. Gopaladas *et al*, 1983; 2. Van Steenbergen *et al*, 1984; 3, Cerqueira *et al*, 1979; NA-not available.

A study on the dietaries of the tribals of Andhra Pradesh revealed a significant variation. The intake of nutrients in the dietaries of pregnant and lactating women were reported to be Calories 1638 and 1700 Kcal, protein 43 and 33 g, calicum 304 and 170 mg, iron 20 and 18 mg, β-carotene 911 and 131 μg respectively (Pratap, 1975).

A dietary study on tribals of East Godavari district reported an intake of, Calories 2206 Kcal, protein 54 g, fat 17 g, β-carotene 344 μg, thiamine 0.82 mg, riboflavin 0.78 mg, niacin 15 mg, vitamin C 211 mg, calcium 418 mg and iron 25 mgs (Pushpamma *et al*, 1983).

Many have reported that the diets of Indian tribes lack in most of the nutrients as compared to the recommended dietary allowances (Roy and Rao, 1971; Sen Gupta, 1960; Sen Gupta and Biswas, 1956; Roy and Rao. 1957; Roy and Rao, 1962; Al-Ani, 1980)

Food and Nutrient intake of tribes outside India

Food intake of the tribes outside India do not seem to be very much different from that of the tribes in India excepting the intake of dairy products and sugars/oils. The per capita intake of several foods by the Fulani herders, a dominant ethinic group in Sahel (Senegalese Ferlo) region in Africa did not vary between July and January months (Benefice *et al*, 1984). The per capita energy intake by Senegalese in differnt months of a year varied from 1892 to 2638 Kcal.

The mean intake of nutrients in the Caribbean tribes is reported to be Calories 2393 Kcal, protein 68 g, calcium 613 mg, iron 15 mg, retinol 954 I.U. thiamine 1.28 mg, riboflavin 1.10, mg, niacin, 15 mg, and vitamin C 60.5 mg (Horner *et al*,1977).

The diets of the lactating women of Iraq tribes of Arab is reported to contain 2293 Kcal, protein 46 g, calcium 87 mg, iron 17mg, vitamin A 1143 IU, thiamine 2.6 mg, riboflavin 1 mg, niacin 78 mg (Al—Ani, 1980).

The diets of the nomads of Iraq is reported to contain 2293 Kcal, protein 46 g, calcium 87 mg, iron 17 mg, vitamin A 1143 I.U. thiamine 1.9 mg, riboflavin 1.5 mg, niacin 18.7 mg and vitamin C 14 mg (Al-Ani, 1980).

Robson and Wadsworth (1977) reported the energy and protein intake of the tribes of low land Circumpolar region to be lower than some tribes living in high land Circumpolar region in Papua New Guinea.

Food and nutrient intake of pre-school children

Limited studies are available on tribal pre-school children dietaries. A study on tribal pre-school children of Srikakulam district reported an intake of 167 g cereals, 30 g pulses, 35 g leafy vegetables, 18 g vegetables, 28 g flesh foods and 12 g milk and milk products. The intake of sugar/jaggery, fats and oils, roots and tubers were found to be negligible (Pratap *et al*, 1976).

The mean dietary intake of nutrients by pre-school children in and outside India (Table 2.5) is found to be much less than the recommended dietary allowances and showed wide variations.

TABLE 2.5

Mean nutrient intake of tribal pre-school children in and outside India

Nutrients	*India*		*Outside India*	
	1	*2*	*3*	*4*
Energy (Kcals)	693	1047	1065	725
Protein (g)	20	34	34	24
Calcium (mg)	312.5	206.0	215.5	282.0
Iron (mg)	16.0	11.99	4.85	6.0
B-carotene (mg)	2884	80.9	252.5	23.8
Thiamine (mg)	0.5	-	1.1	-
Riboflavin (mg)	0.385	-	0.475	-
Niacin (mg)	6.95	-	-	-
Vitamin C (mg)	-	17.47	37.0	-

1. Pratap *et al*, 1976 2. Gopaldas *et al* 1983 3. Van Steenbergen *et al* 1984: 4: Horner *et al*, 1977

Rao and Satyanarayana (1974) studied the nutrient intake of tribal pre-school children of Srikakulam district and the reported average intake of Calories is 750 Kcal and protein 20 g.

NUTRIENT COMPOSITION

Cereals Millets and Legumes

The nutrient composition of cereals, millets and legumes has been examined by a number of scientists in the past. The range of the value reported for proximate composition, minerals and vitamins are presented in Tables 2.6 to 2.9.

Tubers

Nutrient composition of tubers of *Dioscorea* species had been studied by various workers. The Genus *Dioscorea* contains about 600 species that are regarded as edible. The bitter principles present in the roots are said to be removed by soaking and boiling (Gramshaw and Osinowo, 1982).*Dioscorea bulbifera* is reported to be bitter and acrid and can be rendered edible by keeping in the water for 24 hours. The tuber is reported to be less toxic compared to *D.hispida* (Pingale, 1973).

The nutrient composition of several *Dioscroea* species had been studied by various scientists. The range of values reported are protein 0.6 -6.3g, fat 0.04 -0.3g, ash 0.2 - 1.6g, fibre 0.7-1.5g, carbohydrate 5.7-34.1 g. and energy 27 - 131 Kcal. The calcium content of the wild roots ranged from 7 to 57 mg, phosphorus 5 to 275 mg, iron 0.3 to 3.3 mg, thiamine 0.04 to 0.36 mg, riboflavin 0.04 to 0.47 mg, niacin 0.13 to 1.2 mg per cent (Pingale, 1973; Baquar and Oke, 1977; Sen Gupta, 1980; Gopalan *et al*, 1980, Robson *et al 1976)*.

Uncommon foods

The dried bamboo shoots are reported to contain energy 302 Kcal, protein 25.3g, fat 3.3g, fibre 9.5g, carbohydrate 42.8g. calcium 208mg, phosphorus 569mg, iron 12.5mg, riboflavin 0.09mg and niacin 3.8mg per

Pingale (1973) reported the values for caryota palm pith to be very low in protein (0.62g.) fat (0.2g), ash (1.7g), high fibre (10.9g) and carbohydrate (79.3 g). Robson *et al* (1976) in their study on caryota palm pith reported almost similar value as Pingale (1973). The vitamin content of the pith was not reported by the two scientists.

TABLE 2.6

Range of values for proximate composition of cereals and millets reported by several investigators

Foods	Proximate Principles							Studies
	moisture g	Protein g	Fat g	Ash g	Fibre g	Carboh-ydrate g	Calories g	
Rice	7.5-11.5	6.4–15.2	0.1–2.9	0.2–1.6	0.2–0.8	71–79	346	Ambegaokar, 1964; Wahid *et al*, 1981; Deosthale and Pant, 1970; Taira. 1971; Gopalan *et al*, 1980; Swair *et al*, 1978; Dutta and Barua, 1978; Sen Gupta 1980; Wills *et al*, 1982; Rajalaxmi, 1981.
Sorghum	9.9–14.1	7.8–13.8	1.0–3.4	1.2–1.6	0.4–2.0	71–73	349	Oria *et al*, 1975; Hulse *et al*, 1980; Rao and Deosthale, 1980; Maxson *et al*, 1973; Gopalan *et al*, 1980; Jambunathan *et al*, 1984.
Bajra	7.8–15.3	5.8–15.2	2.8 7.9	1.1–2.5	1.1–2.0	54 69	361	Goswami *et al*, 1970; Varriano-Martson and Hoseney, 1980; Goswami *et al*, 1969; Opoku *et al*, 1980; Gopalan *et al*, 1980.
Ragi	12.0–15.6	5.6–11.6	1.5–3.5	2.4–4.0	3.0–4.1	63–74	328	Deosthale *et al*, 1970; Malleshi and Desikachar, 1981; Kurien, 1967; Wankhede *et al*. 1979; Sen Supta, 1980.
Minor millets	6.9–12.2	6.4–18.7	2.9–4.7	1.4–3.8	0.8–8.0	61–79	331	Lorenz *et al*, 1976; Ambegaokar *et al*, 1964; Viswanath and Gajanan, 1979; Sen Gupta, 1980; Lorenz *et al*, 1980; Montiro *et al*, NIN, 1983.
Rajkeera seeds	10.0	12.5–19.4	5.3–8.1	2.0–5.2	2.0–7.2	62–67	364	Connor *et al*, 1981; Abdi and Sahib, 1976; Osuntogun and Oke, 1983; Becker *et al*, 1981; Afolabi *et al*, 1981; Hulse *et al*, 1980 Kurien, 1967.

TABLE 2.7

Range of values for mineral and vitamin content of cereals and millets reported by several investigators

Foods *mg*	*Calcium*	*Phosphorus* *mg*	*Iron* *mg*	*Thiamine* *mg*	*Niacin* *mg*	*Studies*
Rice	10 - 58	30 – 494	0.20- 5.55	0.57- 0.87	1.6– 5.0	Deosthale and Pant, 1970; Soaad *et al*, 1981; Deosthale *et al*, 1979; Dutta and Barua, 1978; Sen Gupta 1980; Gopalan *et al*, 1980.
Sorghum	6 - 32	124 – 223	3.7 15.0	0.21– 0.50	3.1 3.5	Rao and Deosthale, 1980; Rao *et al*, 1958; Hulse *et al*, 1980; Oria *et al*, 1977; Gopalan *et al*, 1980.
Bajra	25 - 132	296 – 410	3.0- 9.2	0.30- 0.58	1.8 2.4	Hulse *et al*, 1980; Deosthale *et al*, 1971; Sen Gupta, 1980; Gopalan *et al*, 1980; Balley *et al*, 1979.
Ragi	15 - 661	283	1.3- 22.8	0.10- 0.66	0.1 4.5	Deosthale *et al*, 1970; Sen Gupta, 1980; Pore and Magar, 1977; Mallanna and Rajaskhara, 1969; Gopalan *et al*, 1980; Varriano-Martson and Honseney, 1980;
Minor millets	12—31	30 – 290	9.4- 19.8	0.04- 0.59	0.4- 3.2	Ambergaokar, 1964; Sen Gupta, 1980; Gopalan, *et al*, 1980; NIN, 1983.
Rajkeera seeds	223– 2850	665	17.6- 106.0	0.17	3.6	Becker *et al*, 1981; Gopalan *et al*, 1980.

TABLE 2.8

Range of values for proximate composition of pulses reported by several investigators

Foods	*Protein* g	*Fat* g	*Ash* g	*Fibre* g	*Carbohydrate* g	*Calories* Kcal	*Studies*
Radgram	15.1-31.5	1.2-3.1	3.3-4.7	1.0-7.0	66 - 69	304	Sharma *et al*, 1977; Rao and Belavady, 1977; Shobhana *et al*, 1976; Singh *et al*, 1984; Jambunathan *et al*, 1984.
Greengram	23.0-30.3	0.96-4.9	3.3-4.1	3.3-8.2	53 - 66	306	Shehta and Thannoun, 1981; Watson, 1977; Kadwe *et al*, 1974; Rao and Belavady, 1979; Shobhana *et al*, 1976.
Blackgram	22.0-28.8	1.0-3.0	3.2-4.4	3.6-4.7	56 - 66	320 334	Kadwe *et al*, 1974; Rao and Belavady, 1979; Pushpama, *et al*, 1983; Shobhana, *et al*, 1976; Watson, 1977; Shehta and Thannoun, 1981; Gopalan, *et al*, 1980.
Horsegram	19.9-26.2	0.5-2.8	2.8-6.4	5.3	5.7 - 59	321	Manage and Sohonie, 1972; Kadwe *et al*, 1974; Vasi and Sai, 1976; Gopalan *et al*, 1980.
Field beans	21.9 27.2	0.7-0.8	2.9-3.2	1.4-4.2	54 - 60	347	Srihara, 1976; Salimath and Tharanthan, 1982; Gopalan *et al*, 1980.
Cowpea	21.2-33.0	1.0-3.0	2.0-5.0	2.0-6.9	54 - 68	321-323	Kadwe, *et al*, 1974; Ologhobo and Fetuga, 1984; Longe, 2980; Meiner *et al*, 1967a; Elias, *et al*, 1964; Gopalan *et al*, 1980; Akpapunum and Markakis, 1979.

TABLE 2.9

Range of values for mineral and vitamin content of pulses reported by several investigators

	Calcium mg	*Phosphorus mg*	*Iron mg*	*Thiamine mg*	*Niacin mg*	*Studies*
Redgram	49 - 276	206 - 618	2.4- 8.3	0.15- 0.45	0.2- 2.8	Sharma *et al*, 1977; Singh *et al*, 1984; Deosthale and Rao, 1981; Kadwe *et al*, 1974; Pushpamma *et al*,, 1983; Sen Gupta, 1980; Gopalan *et al*,, 1980.
Greengram	100 - 200	326 - 795	5.0- 43.0	0.11- 0.49	2.1	Shehta and Thannoun, 1981; Watson, 1977; Kadwe *et al*, 1974; Pushpamma *et al*, 1983; Rao and Belavady, 1979; Rao and Belavady, 1979; Gopalan *et al*, 1980
Blackgram	135 - 350	332 - 1005	2.0- 22.0	0.44-	0.1 0.4	Shehta and Thannoun, 1981; Kadwe, *et al*, 1974; Pushpamma *et al*, 1983; Shobhana *et al*, 1976; Watson, 1977; Rao and Belavady, 1979.
Horse gram	150 - 790	150 - 790	8.0 70.5	0.42	1.5	Gopalan *et al*, 1980; Manage and Sohonie, 1972; Giri *et al*, 1981; Kadwe *et al*, 1974; Pore, 1979.
Field bean	38 - 60	27 - 433	2.7- 6.8	0.52	1.8	Srihara, 1976; Gopalan *et al*, 1980.
Cowpea	69 - 150	400 - 608	5.9- 21.51	0.11- 2.51	1.3- 3.2	Kadwe *et al*, 1974; Meiners *et al*,1976; Meiners *et al*,1976a; Ologhobo and Fetuga, 1984; Murthy *et al*,1965; Gopalan *et al*, 1980.

The uncommon legume (*Mucuna pruriens*) seeds mature during September-November. The proximate composition of this is reported to be rich in protein (29.19 g) and in fibre (10.9 g) (Pingale, 1973).

The *Agaricus* sp. of mushrooms is reported to grow on dead bamboo and available during the months of June through September. Maria Gonds are reported to sun-dry and store them in powdered form to be used as a flavouring agent in various food preparations. The proximate composition of dried mushroom (Agricus sp.) is reported to be rich in protein (26.1g), ash (7.7 g) and fibre (6.9 g) (Pingale, 1973). A higher content of protein (47.4 g) had been reported by Kurtzman (1975).

FOOD PROCESSING

Culinary practices vary from one place to another even from house to house. Nutrient losses on cooking depend on conditions of cooking and on the stability of nutrients. It is partly due to extraction and destruction in the process of cooking. Cooking is said to have both beneficial and adverse effects depending on various methods adopted during cooking.

Effect on vitamin content of cereals and millets

Vitamin losses especially thiamine and riboflavin are reported to be more by wet cooking but no considerable losses in niacin content is reported (Rajayalakshmi, 1981; Pushpamma *et al*, 1983 and Aliya and Geervani, 1981). Fermentation is reported to increase the thiamine content (Pushpamma *et al*, 1983). A study on bajra and ragi by Aliya and Geervani (1981) revealed that fermentation of ragi flour for 24 hours increases thiamine by 58 per cent and decreases by 16 per cent after cooking. However, in cooked product of bajra fermented for 24 hours, thiamine content is reported to be increased by 84 per cent. It was therefore speculated that bajra batter may act as a favourable substrate for synthesis of vitamin B-compounds or alternately the micro-organism present in bajra batter may be different.

Effect on *in vitro* protein digestibility

Various scientists have reported that dehusking had favourable effect on IVPD (Ramachadra *et al*, 1977; Singh and Jambunadhan, 1981; Hulse *et al*, 1980; Chibber *et al*, 1980). The level of tannin content in the grain is reported to influence IVPD (Hulse *et al*, 1980). It had been reported that sorghum with a tannin content of 1.1 to 1.55 mg/100 g showed an IVPD of 27.9 per cent and those with tannin content of 0.9 mg has an IVPD of 60.83 per cent. In grains with tannin content of 0.28 to 0.46 mg/100 g the mean IVPD is reported as 77.3 per cent, indicating an inverse correlation between IVPD and tannin content. A study on unfermented and fermented cooked gruels of sorghum revealed that unfermented cooked gruels has an IVPD of 44 to 56 per cent and fermented cooked gruels has 65 to 86 per cent respectively indicating the beneficial effects of fermentation on IVPD (Axtell *et al*,1981).

Parboiling is reported to have deleterious effect on IVPD of cereals. It is reported that due to parboiling, the un-bound lipid and free fatty acid in milled rice decreases whereas, lipid bound to starch and protein and free phenolic acid increases, thereby reducing the extractibility of protein in the grains (Kato *et al*, 1983).

The IVPD of pearl millet flour was reported to be 75.6 per cent and baking is reported to have no significant effect on IVPD of bajra (Sawaya *et al*, 1984)

Varietal and locational differnces are said to influence IVPD.A study on 13 varieties of finger millet showed a range of 55 to 88 per cent in IVPD (Ramachandra *et al*, 1977). Hulse *et al*, (1980) reported that African x Indian sorghum varieties had 84 per cent digestibility whereas African varieties alone are reported to be 66 per cent digestible. Sorghum and rice grown in Gujarat is reported to have an IVPD of 8.55 and 8.95 per cent respectively. Axtell *et al* (1981) reported an IVPD of 78 to 100 per cent in uncooked sorghum and 45 to 55 per cent in cooked sorghum.

The method followed in the estimation of IVPD are also said to cause variations in the values. A study on rice reported an IVPD of 88 per cent using pepsin and pancreatin and 90 per cent with pepsin and 46 per cent with pancreatin and 47 per cent with pronase. Combination of pepsin and pancreatin showed a high correlation of 0.87 with *in vivo* data whereas poor correlation was reported with pepsin system alone (Hulse *et al*, 1980; Akeson and Stahmann, 1964)

Effect on IVPD of pulses

Various scientists reported an improvement in protein digestibility upon heating in all the pulses due to destruction of growth inhibitors (Friedman, 1975; Devadas *et al*,1964; Singh and Jambunathan, 1981; Singh *et al* 1984; Rao *et al*, 1964; Ray 1971). Satwardhar *et al*(1981) reported an IVPD of 80 per cent for un-cooked horsegram. Another study by Elfaki *et al*(1984) showed an IVPD of 78.6 and 84 per cent for raw and cooked horsegram respectively. Subbulakshmi *et al* (1976) reported an IVPD of 56 and 80 per cent for the raw and cooked horsegram respectively. Jambunathan *et al*(1984) reported an IVPD of 52.5 to 62.0 per cent (mean 59.2) and Kuppuswamy (1958) reported an IVPD of 60 per cent for the uncooked pigeon pea and an IVPD of 79 and 83 per cent for raw and cooked cowpeas. It was reported that the light brown and white samples of raw cowpea seeds have an IVPD range of 75 to 77.6 per cent and that of the dark and red black accessions had an IVPD of 70.8 to 74.5 per cent. Laurena *et al*(1984) reported that condensed tannins localized in the seed coat are positively correlated with seed coat colour which varied from white to light brown. Dark red and black cowpea varieties resulted in the large difference in IVPD (Kuppuswamy, 1958). It has been reported that polyphenolic compounds exhibited a highly significant positive correlation with trypsin and negative correlation with chymotrypsin inhibitor activities resulting in larger differences in IVPD (Singh and Jambunathan (1981).

Effect on trypsin inhibitor content of pulses

For many years it has been recognised that pulses contain trypsin inhibitor and cooking or some other form of heat treatment improved the nutritive value and protein digestibility by destroying them (Meiner, *et al* 1976; Rao *et al*,1964; Burr, 1975; Singh and Jambunathan, 1981; Ray, 1971; Subbulaxmi *et al*, 1976; DE Lumen and Salamut,1980). Soaking and boiling is reported to reduce the TIA content due to leaching. A loss of 4 per cent TIA after boiling for one hour and a loss of 99 per cent in husked beans after heating for 24 hours at 100°C is reported indicating the presence of residual tannins which account for heat resistant TIA. However, soaking for 6 hours and boiling for one hour is reported to decrease TIA by at least 95 per cent (DE Lumen and Salamut, 1980; Ekpenyoung and Borchers, 1981)

The TIA values for cowpea and pigeonpea after soaking for 18 hours in 3 liters of water/kg of beans and autoclaved for 0, 15, 30, 45 minutes at 15 1bs pressure at 121°C are reported as 6.7, 2.8, 2.5, 3.0. and 20.9 3.4 1.3, 2.9, per cent respectively indicating the beneficial effects of autoclaving (Elias *et al*,1976).

Trypsin inhibitor content of some legumes as reported by various scientists is given in Table 2.10.

TABLE 2.10

Trypsin inhibitor content of some legumes

Legume	*TIU*	*Study*
Pigeon Pea	87.11 mg protein	Singh *et al*, 1984.
Pigeon Pea	69.4 mg protein	
Pigeon Pea Wild Sp.	127.6 mg protein	Singh and Jambunathan (1981)
Pigeon Pea Wild Sp.	39.83-46.09 µ moles of tyrosine/ ml extract	Singh *et al*, 1977
Pigeon pea	20.9 ml extract	Elias *et al*, 1976.
Cowpea (Nigeria Sp.10)	6. ml extract	
Greengram	192.8 ml extract	Gupta and Wagle
Blackgram	210.6 ml extract	(1978)
Horsegram Uncooked	50.2 g seed x 10^3	
Horsegram cooked (soaked for 4 hrs Cooked for 40-60 mts)	0.9 g seed x 10^3	Subbulaxmi *et al*, (1976)

CHAPTER 3

MATERIALS AND METHODS

The study comprised a field survey of tribal families, diet survey of women and children and nutrient analysis of foods collected from the tribal households.

FIELD STUDY

Selection of the area

Vizianagaram district in Andhra Pradesh, which has 1.53 lakh tribal population was selected for the study. Out of total 14 Panchayat Samithis in the district two Samithis namely Bhadragiri and Pachipenta agency blocks were selected. Bhadragiri is bordered by Orissa state on the North, Seethampet on the East, Kurupam on South and Parvathipuram on the West. There is no urban area in the block. Pachipenta is bounded by Salur towards North, Gajapathipuram towards South, Salur Samithi on the East and Orissa state in the West. The present study was carried in the two agency blocks where the tribal population of the district is concentrated.

Selection of the tribes

Several tribes live in the two blocks. Therefore, based on the concentration of various tribes (obtained from 1981 records of the Panchayat Samithis) four major tribes namely Jatapu, Savara (from Bhadragiri block), Kondadora and Gadaba tribes (from Pachipenta block) were selected for the study.

Selection of villages and households

List of villages under each tribe was obtained from the respective offices of Panchayat Samithis and selection of village was done by simple

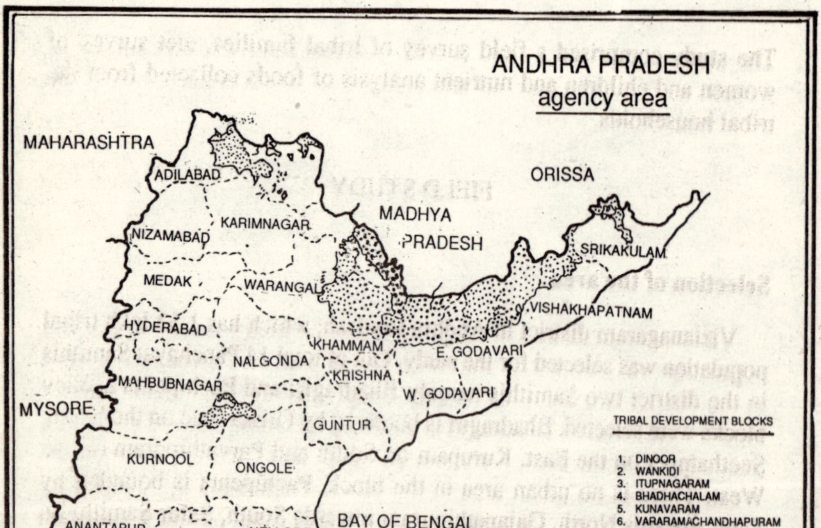

FIG.1. Blocks selected for the study from Vizianagaram District of Andhra Pradesh.

random sampling procedures. Thus six villages each from Jatapu and Savara tribes and four vilalges each from Kondadora and Gadaba tribes were studied.

With regard to selection of households all the available households at the time of visit were covered. Thus the general survey covered 75 families from each of the four tirbes amounting to 300 households. The list of villages, tribes and number of families surveyed are given in Table 3.1.

Collection of general information

A personal interview schedule was designed, pretested and refined for the collection of information. A copy of the schedule is given in Appendix I. The aspects covered include demography, occupation, agricultural and storage practices, infant feeding practices, attitudes, and dietary practices in health and in specific physiological conditions *etc*. The general information was collected interviewing personally both the head of the houshold and his wife.

Morbidity data for one year period from January 1983 to January 1984 was obtained from the records of primary health centres in the two blocks.

Diet survey

General meal combination of the tribals was obtained from the housewives recording the foods consumed the previous day. For the study of the actual dietary intake, women of child bearing age (15-45 yr) and pre-school children (1-6 yr) were selected randomly. Fifty five women from each of Jatapu and Svara tribes and thirty women each from Kondadora and Gadaba tribes and 15 children from each of the four tribes were studied. The information abcut the total quantity of raw foods and cooked food prepared for the family and the individual intake of the cooked foods by the women and pre-school children was collected using a set of standardized vessels, and the raw amount of foods taken by an individual was calculated using the following formula :

$$\text{Amount of raw food consumed by the individual} = \frac{\text{Total raw quantity of food used for family}}{\text{Total cooked quantity of the food}} \times \text{Individual intake of the cooked portion}$$

TABLE 3.1
Data on tribes, villages and families surveyed

Block	*Tribes*	*Villages*	*Distance from head-quarters Km*	*Total number of household as in the records*	*Number of families surveyed*	*Number of families from which food samples were obtained*
	Jatapu	Regidi+	30	22	10	10
		Jatapu+	5	80	16	5
		Kotopadu colony				
		Manda*	12	70	16	6
		Marripalli+*	15	20	10	10
		Rastakuntubai	15	30	12	5
		Kosangibhadra+	20	30	11	5
Bhadragiri Block	Savara	Tikkabai*	18	30	12	7
		Sadunuguda**	8	25	10	6
		Savara Kotapadu*+ colony	6	72	30	5
		Kannyaguda*	7	20	9	6
		Dhulikuppa+	5	12	5	6
		Konaguda*+	5	22	9	8
	Kondadora	Kuntam Bade Valasa**	10	15	8	5
		Ethamanu Valasa++	6	58	27	5
		Puligantu Valasa**	8	25	13	6
		Pindrangi Valasa++	3	52	27	5
Panchipenta	Gadaba	Gadabadbodda Valasa	9	40	11	5
		Kottavalasa	24	70	27	10
		Panukuvalasa	12	65	25	10
		Pedacheepuru Valasa	15	50	12	6

* Wild roots were collected from these villages.
** The villages on the hilly slopes
\+ The villages located in interior areas.
++ The villages on the lower region of the hills

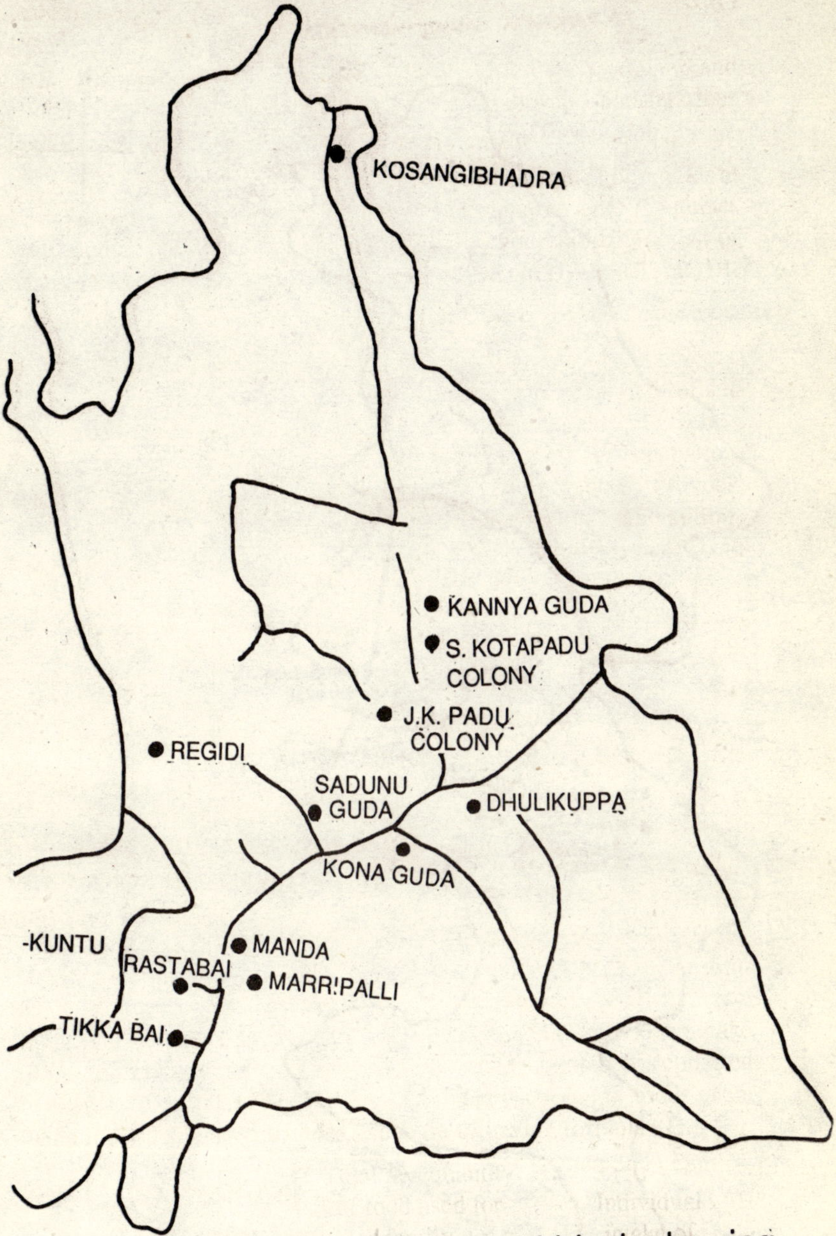

FIG. 2. Map of Bhadragiri block showing the villages selected for the study.

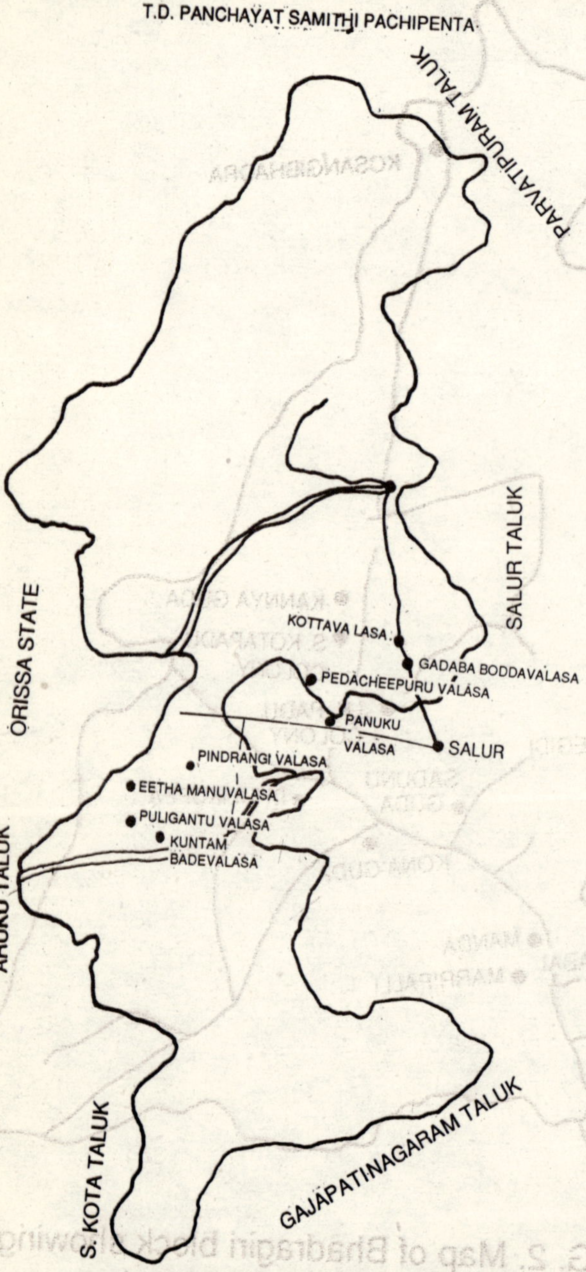

FIG. 3. Map of Pachipenta Block showing the villages selected for the study.

Having thus known the raw portion consumed by the individual, the intake of nutrients from the diets was calculated using food composition tables obtained from actual nutrient analysis of the food consumed by the tribals. In calculating nutrients of perishables-vegetables and flesh foods which were not analysed in the present study, the values of Indian foods published by Gopalan *et al* (1980) were used.

LABORATORY ANALYSIS

Procurement of the foods

Foods commonly consumed by the tribals were collected from 5-10 households at random from all the villages surveyed in the following quantities : cereals/millets/legumes, 100-250 g, wild tubers 500 g -2000 g and miscellaneous foods, 50-200 g. The collection of foods was done thrice (in September, December, February-March) during the period from September 1982 to March 1983, in order to cover most of the available foods consumed by the tribals. Wild tubers were collected from 6 villages as indicated in Table 3.1 where they were available from the nearby forest. Two food products, namely gingelly seed cake and blackgram crisps were collected in the quantity of 50-100 g from 5 to 6 vendors at random. The foods thus collected were pooled/cleaned and sealed in polythene bags, and stored in deep freeze at 0^{0}c for about one week to ten days, till the time of analysis. Roots were stored at room temperature.

The list of foods collected from the tribal households and analysed for their nutrients are presented in Tables 3.2, 3.3 and 3.4.

Preparation of food for nutrient analysis

Cereals and millet grains samples were dehusked in the laboratory following exactly the same procedures as that of the tribals. Legumes were not dehusked as they are mostly consumed whole by the tribals.

Key to Figure 4 (illustration 9)

7.1. Mango pieces (dried)

7.2. a) Tamarind stored as it is;

TABLE 3.2

Cereals and millets collected from the tribals and analysed for their nutrients

Local Name	Description of the sample	Common Name	Scientific Name
1. Gantelu.			
a) Pittagante	Local variety	Bajra	*Pennisetum*
b) Sarkaru Gante	Hybrid variety	pearl millet	*typhoideum*
2. Korra			
a) Veldulu	a) parboiled	Italian millet	*Setaria italica*
b) Uppullu	b) raw	Foxtail millet	
3. Jonna			
a) Tella	white	Jowar	*Sorghum vulgare*
b) Yerra	red		
4. Alu/Arika	Plain land grown	Varagu	*Paspalum*
		Kodo millet	*scrobiculatum*
5. Ooda (Uppullu)	Parboiled	Sanwa millet	*Echinochloa*
			frumentacea
6. Tydalu/chollu		Ragi	*Eleusine coracana*
		Finger millet	
a) Tella chodi	Dark reddish		
b) punasa chodi	Medium colour		
c) Buroda chodi	Light colour		
7. Biyyam	a) raw hand pound	Rice	*Oryza sativa*
	b) Parboiled and hand pound		
	c) Red rice		
8. Sama	Parboiled	Samai Little millet	*Panicum miliare*

TABLE 3.3

Legumes collected from the tribals and analysed for their nutrients

Local Name	Description of the sample	Common name	Scientific name
1. Minumulu	Green colour	Blackgram	*Phoseolus mungo*
2. Bobbarlu	Dryland grown	Cowpea	*Vigna catjang*
3. Chikkudu			
a) Nalla	Black variety	Field bean	*Dolichos lablab*
b) Tella	White variety		
c) Sinama	Red variety		
4. Judumulu/Junumulu	hill grown		*Vigna sp.*
5. Ulavalu			
a) Tella ulavalu	White variety	Horsegram	*Dolichos biflorus*
b) Nalla ulavalu	Black variety		
6. Kandi			
a) Podukandi	(a) Dryland grown	Redgram	*Cajanus cajan*
b) Sirikandi	(b) hill grown	hill grown	
7. Dukka chikkudu or Dukka pikka	a wild bean		*Mucuna pruriens*

TABLE 3.4
Wild tubers and miscellaneous foods collected from the tribals and analysed for their nutrients

Local Name	*Description of the sample*	*Common name*	*Scientific name*
1. Arika tega	tuber	not known	*Dioscorea oppositifolia*
2. Chedu dumpa	tuber	not known	*D. bulbifera*
3. Pandimukku tega	tuber	not known	*D. pentaphylla*
4. Pulidumpa	tuber	not known	*D. hispida*
5. Veduru kanje	cut into long thin pieces, boiled and sun-dried	Bamboo shoot	*Bambusa arundinacea*
6. Veduru kokku	Wildly grown on dead bamboo (sun-dried)	Mushroom	*Agaricus Sp.*
7. Jillugu pindi	prepared from caryota palm pith	Caryota palm pith	*Caryota urens*
8. Rajanala	hill grown	Rajkeera seeds	*Amaranthus paniculatus*
9. China vadialu	cooked product made from black gram flour (dried)	Black gram crisps	*Pheseolus mungo*
10. Pindi vadialu	a product made with whole defatted gingelly cake.	Til cake products	Sesamum indicum whole

b) with turmeric and salt;

c) with salt alone.

7.3 Bamboo shoots (tender) (processed and dried). 7.4 Mushroom (dried)

7.5 Mahuva flowers (dried). 7.6 Zillugu pindi. 7.7 mango stones and its powder. 9.1 Herbal balls used in the preparation of millet beer.

Key to Figure 5 (illustration 8)

8.1. Blackgram crisps. 8.2. Gingelly vadialu. 8.3 *Varragunda* (powder made of chillies coriander seeds garlic, pepper).

A representative portion from the pooled lot was taken for analysis of nutrients, by sub-sampling. The samples were then powdered in a stainless steel grinder and mixed thoroughly to ensure equal distribution. Tubers were peeled and cut using a stainless steel knife and mashed well in a stainless steel grinder to avoid metal contamination.

FOOD PROCESSING

Dehusking of Cereals and Millets

Paddy and millets were dehusked by the dry processing methods involving direct pounding of the grains. The millets, bajra and jowar were dehusked by wet processing method sprinkling 200 to 250 ml water to 4 kgs of the grain at the time of pounding. The yield of the grain after processing was 700 to 800 g per 1 kg.

Tribals have the habit of parboiling new grains especially *sama* (*Panicum miliare*) *ooda*, (*Echinocloa colona var-frumentacea*), korra (*setaria italica*), and paddy (*Oryza sativa*). The grain is boiled in a covered pot for about an hour till the water is completely absorbed by the grains. For 5 to 6 kg of grain 2000 ml to 3000 ml water was used.

The parboiled grains then were spread on a flat bamboo woven mat-like structure locally known as '*Dangari*' and dried in shade prior to sundrying. The parboiled grains were locally known as '*uppullu*'. They are stored for about 1 to 3 months by the tribals and the grains are dehusked in small quantities when required.

For the purpose of the present study, the parboiled millets *sama*, *ooda* and *korra* were collected directly from the tribals at random and were dehusked in the laboratory and then were used for the preparation of products in the laboratory.

Cooking of the cereals and millets

Boiling is common in the cooking procedure adopted by the tribals. The grain is washed twice before cooking and added to the boiling water and cooked. Cereal/millet preparations are cooked in large amounts of water (in the ratio of 1:5) in the nights and extra water drained and preserved. Combination products of millets and rice (4:1) are also commonly consumed by the tribals. In this case, rice is added to the half boiled millet and cooked. The left over rice after dinner is mixed with the *conjee* drained and kept overnight to be taken as morning meal. Cooking is done using mud pot and firewood. All the food preparations were standardized prior to actual selection for analysis.

Cereal/millet products were prepared in the laboratory just as tribals did and analysed for nutrients. The products were as follows.

a. Bajra and rice product.

b. *korra* and rice product.

c. *Korra* (*veldulu*) product: dehusked korra was used for the preparation of the product.

d. *korra* (*uppullu*) product: parboiled and dehusked *korra* was used.

f. Jowar product : whole dehusked jowar was used.

e. *Ooda* (*uppullu*) product: parboiled and dehusked grain was used.

g. Rice product : Raw rice was used in making the products.

h. Ragi gruel : Ragi was pounded and dehusked and ground to flour in stone *chakki*. Prior to actual preparation, the flour was soaked with adequate amounts of water. A small quantity of bajra bran was added to it and allowed for fermentation for 18-24 hours keeping the pot covered with a lid. For the actual preparation, water was boiled in a pot and the fermented ragi batter was poured slowly into the boiling water mixing simultaneously to avoid lump formation, and cooked till done and removed from fire.

1. Bajra Gruel.

It is also prepared in the same way using bajra flour, but the fermentation step is omitted.

The processing particulars of cereals/millets are given in Table 3.5.

TABLE 3.5

Cooking time and weight of cooked cereals and millets

Preparation	*Weight *of the raw food (g)*	*Weight* of the cooked food (g)*	*Cooking* time hr-mts*	*Conjee* left over ml*
Bajra and rice product	300	660	0-16	170
korra and rice product	300	750	0-20	250
korra (raw) product	300	660	0-18	160
korra(parboiled) product	300	750	0-18	350
Ooda product	300	720	0-27	300
Jowar product	300	1080	0-20	150
Rice product	300	1065	0-15	150
Ragi gruel	100	750	0-15	-
Bajra gruel	100	250	0-12	-

*Mean of three values.

Portioning for nutrient analysis :

Primarily the food material was made into 4 equal portions, one portion (300 g) was kept aside for estimation of nutrients in the raw sample, the remaining three portions (300 g each) were cooked separately, and each of the cooked product was divided into two equal portions. To one portion the left over *conjee* is added, and kept overnight. The raw, cooked and the samples kept overnight thus obtained (in triplicate) were pooled and mashed separately in a stainless steel grinder. For estimating the thiamine and niacin, the required ground portion was kept aside and the analysis was carried out immediately. The remaining portions of the cooked products were dried at 500°C to 60°C overnight and powdered in mortar and pestle. The powdered samples were then estimated for protein digestibility *in vitro*.

Preparation of pulses for nutrient analysis

Three lots of each type of pulses (9) were weighed. A portion (60g) from each lot was kept aside for analysis of nutrients in the raw state. The remaining two portions (60 g each) were cooked separately with adequate amounts of water. No prior soaking was done (The ratio of pulse to water used was 1:10). The legumes were cooked till soft when pressed between fingers. In case of *dukka chikkudu*, a toxic legume, special processing was required. Boiling and draining was carried out several times till the liquid appeared milky white. The processing details of the legumes are given in Table 3.6.

TABLE 3.6

Cooking time and weight of cooked pulses

Legume	*Initial* weight of raw food taken (g)*	*Cooked* weight of raw fod food (g)*	*Cooking Time* of the unsoaked food (hr-mts)*
Horsegram white	60	148	2-05
Horsegram black	60	138	2-20
Judumulu	60	170	0-50
Redgram (*podu*-cultivated)	60	158	2-05
Dukka chikudu	60	106	8-hours**
Field bean white	60	142	1-10
Field bean red	60	152	1-30
Cowpea (green)	60	142	0-55

* Mean of two values.

** This legume required a period of eight hours of processing involving boiling in water and draining till the colour of the cooking water changed from the original black to whitish colour.

The boiled legumes were drained and dried overnight in an oven at 50°C to 60°C and powdered in stainless steel grinder for estimation of protein digestibility *in vitro*.

ANALYTICAL STUDIES

The foods were analysed for various nutrients following the methods given as follows :

The proximate principles : Moisture, protein (N x 6.25) crude fat (either extractives), ash and crude fibre were estimated according to the standard AOAC (1975) methods. The carbohydrate content was calculated by difference. Energy value was calculated.

Minerals: Iron (colorimetric) and phosphorus (fluorometric) were determined following AOAC (1975) procedures. Calcium (titrimetric) was estimated as described by Hawk *et al* (1957).

Thiamine was estimated using modified thiochrome method of Leveille, 1972 as modified by Ramasastry, 1976.

Riboflavin and niacin were determined microbiologically using *L. casei* and *L. arabinosis*, respectively following AOAC (1975) procedures.

Total starch content was estimated by digesting the sample with glucoamylase (Sigma) and the amount of glucose was determined by phenol-sulphuric acid reaction (Dubois *et al*, 1956).

In vitro digestibility of starch was determined by using α-amylase (Sigma) (Kon *et al*, 1971). Amylase inhibitor activitiy in the tubers was analysed using the method of Jaffe *et al*, (1973).

Trypsin inhibitor content of the pulse was estimated by using the method described by Kakade *et al*, (1969).

In vitro digestibility of protein was determined using pepsin (Sigma) and pancreatin (Loba) as described by Akeson and Stahmann (1964). The protein was precipitated with 10% TCA and Nitrogen content was estimated by microkjeldhal method using the calculations as, Nitrogen in the TCA supernatent corrected for blank divided by nitrogen in the sample extract x 100.

STATISTICAL ANALYSIS

Analysis of variance (one way classification) (Snedecor and Cochran, 1967) was done to find out the significant difference (at 5% level) in the dietary intake of nutrients among the four tribes. Standard deviation of the food and nutrient intake of the women and children was calculated.

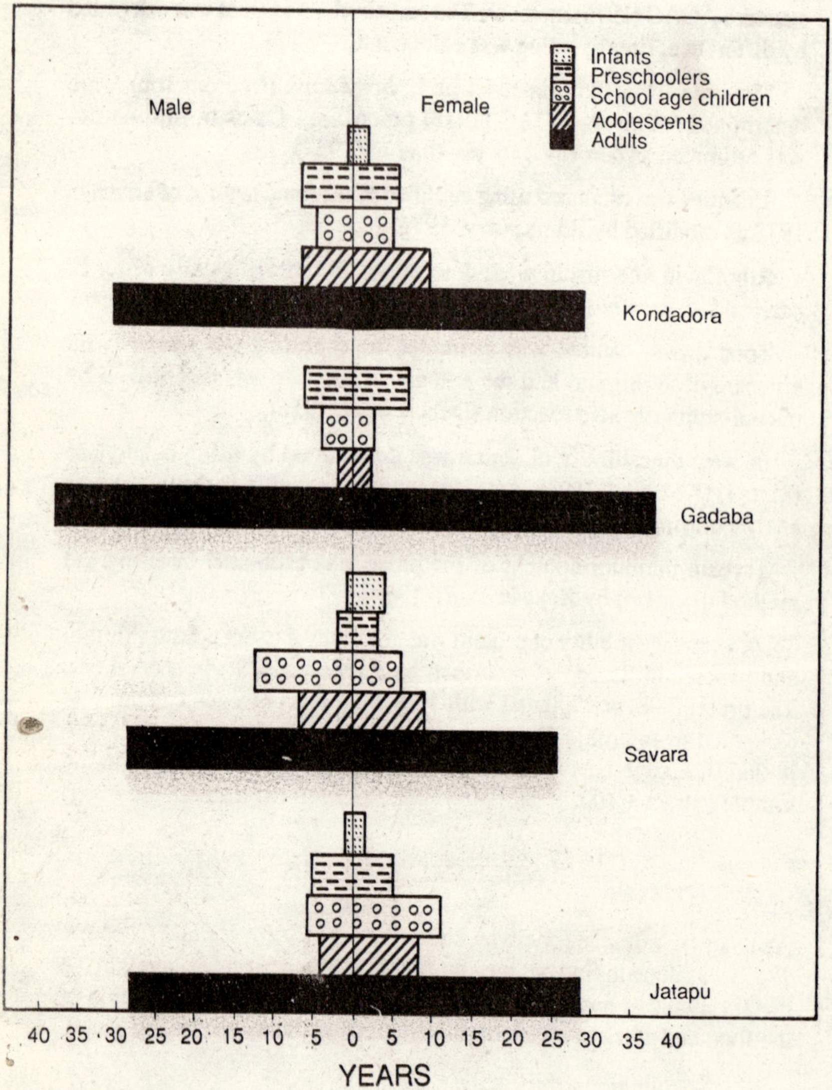

FIG. 6. Sex and Age wise distribution of Tribals Surveyed

CHAPTER 4

FINDINGS

The study covered several areas related to the tribal population, and this helps in understanding their demography, socio-economic condition, food and nutrient intake, nutrient composition, and food processing practices. The results obtained are presented in the following sections: (1) Demography and Socio-economic conditions, (2) Food and Nutrient intake, (3) Nutrient composition; and (4) Food processing.

DEMOGRAPHY AND SOCIO-ECONOMIC CONDITIONS

Population and family size

The age and sex distribution of the tribal population of the four selected tribes Jatapu, Savara, Kondadora and Gadaba is presented in Fig. 6.

Population above 20 years constitute 61 per cent, adolescents and school children and pre-school children constitute 13 per cent each. The male to female ratio is 1000:1032. The dependency ratio in the tribes is 26.5 per cent.

Mean family size of the four tribes is given in Table 4.2.

TABLE 4.1

Age-Sex distribution of the population in the four tribes

Group	*Jatapu*		*Savara*		*Gadaba*		*Kondadora*		*Total*		*Grand*
	M	*F*	*M*	*F*	*M*	*F*	*M*	*F*	*male*	*female*	*total*
Adults (>20 years)	95	95	199	89	122	122	117	110	434 (64)	416 (59)	850 (61)
Adolescents (13-19 years)	15	27	25	31	7	7	25	37	72 (10)	102 (15)	174 (13)
School children (7-12 years)	19	37	44	22	13	8	17	20	93 (14)	87 (12)	1180 (13)
Pre-school children (0-6 years)	22	21	12	25	20	22	27	29	81 (12)	97 (14)	178 (13)
Total population									680	702	1382

Dependency ratio: 26.5 per cent

Values in parenthesis represent percentages.

TABLE 4.2

Family size of the tribals surveyed

Family size	*Jatapu*	*Savara*	*Gadaba*	*Kondadora*	*Total*
1-3	15	15	21	14	65(22)
4-5	46	45	44	40	175(58)
6-8	14	15	10	13	532(17)
8-9	—	—	—	8	(3)
Total	75	75	75	75	300(100)

Values in parenthesis represent percentages.

The mean family size of the four tribes is 4.63. But analysis of per cent of families of different family size reveals that the family size of 58 per cent of families is between 4 to 5 and 22 per cent of families is between 1 to 3.

Occupation

Agriculture is the primary occupation of 78 per cent of the families (Table 4.3) and agricultural labour is the secondary occupation of the tribals. For 20 per cent of the families non-agricultural labour is the primary occupation and agricultural labour is the secondary occupation. The families engaged in government jobs form only 2 per cent.

TABLE 4.3

Occupational distribution of the tribal families

Occupation	*Jatapu*	*Savara*	*Gadaba*	*Kondadora*	*Total*
Agriculture as primary and agricultural labour as secondary	62	71	30	71	234(78)
Non-agricultural labour as primary and agricultural labour as secondary	6	4	45	4	59(20)
Government Employment as primary and agriculture as secondary	7	-	-	-	7(2)
				Total	300(100)

Values in parenthesis represent percentages.

Land-holding

The type of landholding of the four tribes is given in Table 4.4.

TABLE 4.4

Type of land-holding of the tribal families

Tribes	*Hill (Shifting) Cultivation*	*Dry land (Settled) Cultivation*		*No land Cultivation*
		Own	Leased	
Jatapu	53	48	1	6
Savara	69	53	—	4
Gadaba	10	20	10	45
Kondadora	58	53	—	4
Total No. of families	190 (63)	174 (58)	11 (3)	59 (20)

Values in parenthesis represent percentages

Podu (hill) cultivation is practised by 63 per cent of tribal families. 58 per cent of the tribal families are engaged in dryland farming. 20 per cent of the families did not have any land of their own for cultivation.

Cropping pattern

Mixed cropping pattern is practised in *podu* cultivation. The seeds are broadcast on the cleared land and attended to only at the time of harvest. Relay cropping pattern is followed in dryland agriculture. Paddy is grown both on hill and in plains where irrigation facilities are available. The major crops grown are paddy, sorghum, bajra, ragi, and other minor millets like *sama*, *ooda*, *korra*, *arika*, pulses redgram, horsegram, cowpea, and cash crops mainly tobacco, turmeric, castor, niger, sesame and groundnut. In spite of the diversity of the food crops cultivated, the crop yields are poor *i.e.*, on an average 2 to 15 quintals in *podu* cultivation and 3 to 10 quintals per hectare in dryland cultivation. Apart from the common crops, the tribals also cultivate a less common cereal like grain namely rajkeera seeds (*Amaranthus paniculatus*) and among legume crops grown *dukka chikkudu* (*Mucuna pruriens*) and *judumulu* are less known.

Food storage

Tribals store the food-grains both for consumption and seed purposes. Information regarding the method of storage, and period of storage of food-grains is given in Tables 4.5 and 4.6 respectively.

TABLE 4.5

Methods of storage of grains by the tribal families

Tribe	*Earthenware pots*	*Baskets*	*Gunny Bags*
Jatapu	72	3	-
Savara	75		-
Gadaba	19	55	1
Kondadora	63	10	2
Total	229 (76)	68 (23)	3 (1)

Values in parenthesis represent percentages.

TABLE 4.6

Period of storage of food grains by the tribal families

Tribe	*Period stored*		*No storage*
	1 year	*1-6 months*	
Jatapu	7	68	—
Savara	15	60	—
Gadaba	—	55	20
Kondadora	22	53	—
Total	44 (15)	236 (78)	20 (7)

Values in parenthesis represent percentages.

Tribals use earthenwares (76 per cent), baskets (23 per cent) and gunny bags (1 per cent) for storing of grains. 78 per cent of the families stored food grains for 1 to 6 months and 15 per cent for one year. 7 per cent did not store any grain.

Sun-drying is the usual pre-treatment adopted before storing of food-grains. However, with regard to redgram stored for seed purposes, special care is taken by a few families (30 per cent). The families mixed ash alone (1 kg/bag) and/or *nalla zeedi* (*Senecarpus anacardium*) seeds to redgram (4 to 6 numbers/bag) prior to storage. Some of the families (18 per cent) mixed neem leaves to redgram before storage.

Among the wild foods collected from forest are caryota palm pith, mango stone, bamboo shoots and mushroom. These are also sun-dried and stored for a year by the tribals.

Tribals store tamarind in three different ways. The common method is: storing it as it is without seeds. Secondly, sprinkling salt water to the pulp and subjecting it to sun-drying and thirdly, adding salt (2 kgs) and turmeric powder (1/4 kg) to 30 kg of pulp made into small balls, cattle meat is also stored by the tribals. Pieces of meat are strung on a fibre and tied over the fire-place for drying or the pieces inserted in between split bamboo and hung high inside the house. The dried pieces are stored for a month in a pot. No salt is added during the process.

Morbidity

It is difficult to get the morbidity data from the families correctly because of difficulty in reaching and communication. Hence, in the present study, morbidity particulars of the cases reported at the local primary health centres (PHC) during the period 1983 January to 1984 January are obtained from the records. The per cent incidence of illness as compared to both the total registered cases and the total population in the two blocks is presented in Table 4.7.

The data indicate high incidence (37 per cent) of scabies/dermatitis followed by infection and infestation. The incidence of anaemia, B-complex deficiency is 6 to 7 per cent. Total cases of the diseases related to eye form 6 per cent and further detailed classification of the diseases related to eye is presented in Table 4.8.

TABLE 4.7

Incidence of morbidity during the year 1983 - 84

Ailments	*Number of cases Registered*	*Per cent to the total registered cases in PHC*	*Per cent to the total population in the two blocks*
Scabies/Dermatitis	3311	37	3.578
Fever	1274	14	1.376
Gastric Disorders	823	9	0.900
Bronchitis	670	8	0.700
B-complex deficiency	657	7	0.710
Anaemia	529	6	0.570
Diseases related to eye	527	6	0.570
Arthritis	507	6	0.550
Otitis	198	2	0.213
Malaria	143	2	0.154
Others	279	3	0.300
Total cases registered	8918	100	9.651

TABLE 4.8

Classification of diseases related to eye as registered in the PHCs

Eye diseases	*Number of cases registered*	*Per cent to the total registered cases*	*Per cent to the total population in the two blocks*
Non-nutritional:			
Conjuctivits	371	70	0.400
Cataract	96	18	0.104
Myopia	47	9	0.050
Total	514	97	0.554
Nutritional:			
Night blindness	6	1.4	0.006
Xerosis	4	0.9	0.004
Bitot Spots	3	0.7	0.003
Total	13	3.0	0.013

It is clear from the Table 4.8 that majority(97 per cent) of the diseases related to eye are found to be of non-nutritional origin and only 3 per cent are of nutritional origin.

DIETARY PATTERN

Consumption of staples

From Table 4.9 it is seen that millet is the staple food for 55 per cent of the families and only 14 per cent consumed rice as staple food. Rice in combination with millets is consumed by 31 per cent of the tribal families.

TABLE 4.9

Staple grain consumption by the tribal families

Staple grains	*Jatapu*	*Savara*	*Gadaba*	*Kondadora*	*Total*
Millet alone	31	59	38	37	165 (55)
Rice and millets	22	8	31	32	93 (31)
Rice alone	22	8	6	6	42 (14)

Values in parentheis represent percentages.

Meal combinations

Tribals used four types of dietary combinations, staple alone with or without tamarind rasam, staple with legume/oilseed cake, staple with vegetables and staple with flesh foods, mainly dryfish and cattle meat. Data have been analysed in rspect of the combination of foods used taken in the morning, noon, and night by the tribal families. The data is presented in Table 4.10.

Most of the tribal families eat staples in combination with vegetables (48 per cent), some (35 per cent) consumed staple along with or without tamarind rasam, 16 per cent consumed staple with legume/oilseed cake and only 1 per cent of families used staple in combination with flesh food.

ATTITUTDES RELATED TO FOOD

Attitudes reflect the tradition or custom of a community. Therefore, information on attitudes of tribal women on weaning, and on dietary practices in general and in specific physiological conditions like pregnancy, lactation are collected.

From Table 4.11 it is evident that 89 per cent of the tribal women suggested 1 to 2 years as the age of weaning and 11 per cent of the women suggested below 1 year of age. Other information of infant feeding practices revealed that colostrum is not discarded and the child is put to breast on the same day after delivery. The child is breast fed upto 2 to 3 years and weaned directy to an adult diet.

Table 4.10
Meal pattern of the tribal families

Meal combinations	*Jatapu n=75*			*Savara n = 75*			*Gadaba n = 75*			*Kondadora n = 75*			*Grand total*
	M	***L***	***D***	***M***	***L***	***D***	***M***	***L***	***D***	***M***	***L***	***D***	
Staple alone with or without tamarind	52	52	30	21	21	20	19	32	14	30	50	8	349 (35)
Staple with legume or oil seed cake	12	11	10	2	2	4	42	2	14	17	17	25	158 (16)
Staple with vegetables	15	12	31	52	51	54	15	57	81	29	10	63	470 (48)
Staple with flesh food	—	—	—	—	—	—	—	—	4	—	—	2	6 (1)

Values in parenthesis represent percentages.
M **: Morning** ***L*** **: Lunch** ***D*** **: Dinner**

TABLE 4.11

Age of weaning the infants in the four tribes

Tribe	Percentage of the women who suggested	
	< 1 year	*1-2 Years*
Jatapu n = 75	4	96
Savara n = 75	-	100
Gadaba n = 75	33	67
Kondadora n = 75	5	95
Total n = 300	11	89

General food beliefs of tribals

In general, inter-tribe differences with regard to group and customs were found to be present. Jatapu from Bhadragiri and Kondadora from Pachipenta block were said to be superior tribes and no intra-tribe marriages are practiced among them. However, the beliefs and food practices of the tribals were found to be the same.

A majority of tribals considers millets to be good compared to rice. Combination products of two different millets with cereal rice are considered good and tasty. Traditional variety of bajra is preferred over hybrid which was also cultivated in the area, as the latter is believed to cause joint pains and diarrhoea. Consumption of freshly harvested grains of paddy, *korra*, *sama* and *ooda* are said to be not good for health but when need arises as in shortage of food grains, the grains are parboiled and eaten.

Rice or millet beer is believed to provide health and vigour to the body and said to produce cooling effect on the body and so consumed in greater quantities, about 3-10 litres in summer. Though fermented ragi gruel is considered good for health and preferred for its sour taste, the product is restricted to people suffering from illness and to lactating women. Among the uncommon foods, *Tenkapindi* (made from dried mango stone) and *mucuna pruriens* are considered good for health wheareas caryota palm pith is said to cause '*vatham*' (body pains). Milking the cow is believed to be a sin but milch cattle is sacrificed for meat. Snakes are consumed by Savara tribe but other tribes abhor it.

Diet during specific physiological conditions

Severe dietary restrictions are followed during illness. The diet mainly consists of rice and tamarind *rasam* (liquid extract boiled with a little salt).

During pregnancy no food restrictions are followed. However, severe food restrictions are practised during lactation period. After delivery, the women are given a ground paste made with asafoetida and jaggery, in small quantities of about betelnut size. It is believed to be good for health and prevents abdominal pain. Lactating women are given boiled and cooled water for drinking. The drinking water is usually boiled with some special ingredients such as *pippallu* (*Piper longum*), *Karakkai* (*myrobalan*), blackpeppers (*Piper nigrum*), *Zeera* (*cuminum cyminum*), mustard seeds (*Brassica nigra*), and roots like *Nalla upperu* (*Vitis quadrangularis*) and *chitramulam* (*Plumbago zeylanicum*) etc., and then filtered. The filtered water known as *pippallu Neellu* is given for drinking for 9 days in place of ordinary water. If *pippallu* water is not tolerated, alternatively water wherein dried bamboo shoot is placed and boiled is given which is believed to cure abdominal pain.

The residue obtained at the time of preparation of *pippallu* water is used, in the preparation of '*pippallu kayakam*', a paste-like mixture obtained by boiling the residue in combination with jaggery. It is given in small amounts to the women for the first 9 days after delivery.

The lactating woman is given bath on 3rd day, with the water previously boiled with some leaves, (*Vailaku*, bamboo leaves, and wild gogu leaves) which is believed to eliminate the body odour and relieve body pains. From 3rd day, food consisting of hot rice, redgram dhal rasam (supernatant liquid obtained after boiling redgram dhal) and '*dhaniya karam*' (powdered mixture of dried coriander seeds, chilli powder and salt) is given twice a day. From 9th day onwards, the same diet is given twice a day. They resume normal diet after 1 to 3 months depending on their economic conditions. Before switching on to the normal diet, a native medicine is taken which is believed to guard from all ill-effects.

Some foods, however, are restricted for lactating women for a period ranging from two months to one year even after resuming of normal diet. The details are as follows:

Among the three varieties of ragi cultivated, *punasa* variety is preferred and given after 1-2 months. Unfermented ragi gruel is considered good for health, in comparison to fermented one. Consumption of bajra is avoided for 3 months as it is believed to make the mother's milk undigestible for the infant. Black coloured horsegram is considered good over white coloured horsegram. Redgram grown in dry land (*Sirikandi*) is preferred over the gram grown on hill.

With regard to restrictions of vegetables, small sized ridgegourd and bottle gourd are preferred over the big ones as the latter is believed to interfere with digestion of mother's milk, by the infant. Brinjal and green leafy vegetables are avoided by the mother for about 6 months for the fear that the child may pass green stools. Pumpkin is believed to cause '*Vatham*' (pains). Tamarind is avoided for about a month as it is believed to delay the cure of child's sore navel. Raw onions are avoided as it is considered to be cold producing. All roots and tubers excepting a wild tuber namely *Arika tega (D. oppositifolia)* are avoided for one year. *Arika tega* is considered to have medicinal value too.

Among the flesh foods, prawns and cock meat are avoided for a year for the fear that the child's neck might be deformed likewise. Except hen's meat, the flesh foods in general are avoided for 5 to 6 months as they are considered not good for health of the mother, and the infant.

Mahua flowers, *Mucuna pruriens*, papaya fruit are considered galactogogues by the tribal women.

FOOD AND NUTRIENT INTAKE

Food and nutrient intake of the women of child-bearing age and preschool children are presented in this section and are compared with recommended dietary allowances for Indians (ICMR, 1981). The mean daily food and nutrient intake of the women as obtained from the help of food composition tables is presented in Tables 4.12 to 4.15.

TABLE 4.12
Food intake of the tribal women

Food (g)	*Jatapu n = 55*	*Savara n = 55*	*Gadaba n = 30*	*Kondadora n = 30*	*Mean*	*% RDA* met*
Cereals/millets	427	433	430	429	429.7	97.7
SD	49.7	63.9	49.7	35.4		
Pulses/Oil seed cake	32	—	33	35	25.7	55.5
SD	17	—	20	20		
Green leafy vegetables	100	60	—	—	47.5	47.5
SD	50	20	—	—		
Vegetables	98	116	120	117	112.7	281.6
SD	18.5	20	40	24.6		
Roots	29	—	30	32	22.7	45.5
SD	15.3	—	20	21	—	—
Flesh foods	25.6	10	25	26.2	19.2	64.0
SD	8.14	2	7.5	8.66		

*Ref. ICMR (1981), *Recommended Dietary intakes for Indians.*

TABLE 4.13

Nutrient intake of the tribal women as compared to the Recommended Dietary Allowances

Nutrients	*Jatapu* $n = 55$	*Savara* $n = 55$	*Gadaba* $n = 30$	*Kondadora* $n = 30$	*Mean*	*%RDA* met*
Energy (Kcal)	1722	1736	1724	1735	1729	78.7
SD	160	150	168	170		
Protein (g)	47.4	40.4	48.8	48.0	46.2	102.6
SD	8.1	7.8	12.5	10.8		
Calcium (Mg)	1159	1199	56	66	620	137.7
SD	52.8	54.4	10.0	11.0		
Iron (mg)	56.5	42.4	39.6	39.4	44.6	139.4
SD	5.2	8.2	6.2	5.2		
β-Carotene(μg)	1159	1199	55.9	66.1	620	20.6
SD	270	280	10.0	12.0		
Vitamin C (mg)	20.5	30.9	20.1	19.9	20.3	50.8
SD	8.20	8.40	5.20	5.20		
Thiamine (μg)	1.02	1.45	1.51	1.41	1.35	122.4
SD	0.160	0.220	0.250	0.340		
Riboflavin (mg)	0.791	0.767	0.853	0.919	0.832	64.0
SD	0.13	0.22	0.05	0.10		
Niacin (mg)	11.63	11.07	16.42	16.3	15.15	92.4
SD	2.80	3.20	4.80	4.50		

ICMR, 1981, *Recommended Dietary intakes for India.*

TABLE 4.14
Food intake of the tribal pre-school children

Food(g)	*Jatapu* $n = 15$	*Savara* $n = 15$	*Gadaba* $n = 15$	*Kondadora* $n = 15$	*Mean*	*%RDA** *met*
Cereals/Millets	230	240	235	232	234	105
SD	33.1	12.4	17.3	14.9		
Pulses/Oil seed cake	10.6	—	10.7	12.3	8.4	2.4
SD	5.8	—	7.5	7.6		
Green leafy Vegetables	—	19.5	—	—	4.9	11
SD	—	5.04	—	—		
Other vegetables	40	38	44.1	43.1	41.3	165
SD	25.5	11.5	28.0	26.4		

* IMCR. 1981, *Recommended Dietary intakes for Indians.*

TABLE 4.15
Nurtient intake of the tribal pre-school children as compared to the Recommended Dietary Allowances

Nutrients	*Jatapu* *n = 15*	*Savara* *n = 15*	*Gadaba* *n = 15*	*Kondadora* *n = 15*	*Mean*	*%RDA* met*
Energy (kcal)	822	826	823	820	823	56.0
SD	50	60	62	73		
Protein (g)	19.1	18.2	19.7	19.3	19.1	74.3
SD	4.1	2.5	4.2	3.8		
Calcium(mg)	76.4	42.6	83.6	81.2	71.0	15.7
Sd	20	10	30	25		
Iron(mg)	16.2	17.3	13.1	13.0	14.9	66.2
SD	2.1	2.9	4.0	3.8		
β-carotene(mg)	193	214	16.4	8.33	108	9.82
SD	50	30	4.1	2.4		
Vitamin C(mg)	8.13	5.86	9.20	2.56	6.43	16.0
SD	2.0	0.9	2.1	10		
Thiamine 9mg)	0.253	0.393	0.626	0.606	0.469	62.5
SD	0.09	0.02	0.08	0.10		
Riboflavin (mg)	0.235	0.198	0.280	0.258	0.242	28.4
SD	0.03	0.04	0.09	0.08		
Niàcin(mg)	3.666	3.6	6.6	6.7	4.89	51.4
SD	0.7	0.5	0.2	0.25		

* ICMR, 1981. *Recommended Dietary intakes for Indians.*

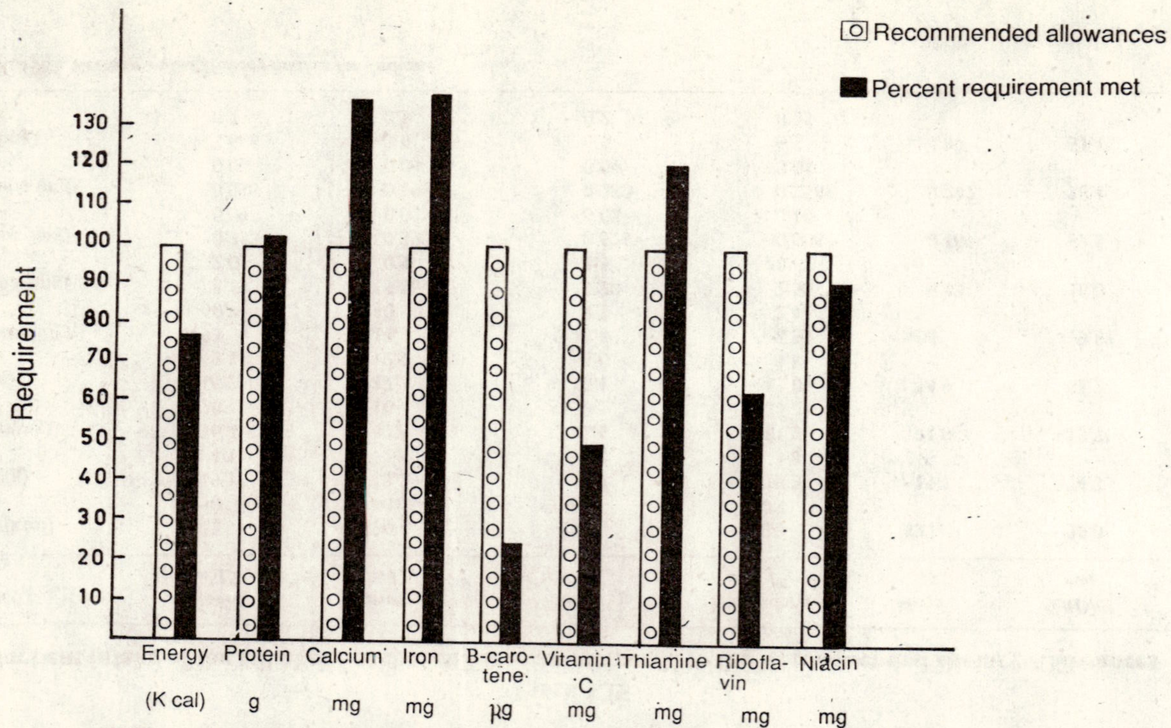

FIG. 7. Percent of Nutrient Requirements met by the Tribal women.

Food and nutrient intake of women

The intake of staple grains by the tribal women is nearly adequate but the consumption of vegetables is almost three times higher as compared with RDA. The intake of pulses/oilseeds, green leafy vegctables, root vegetables and flesh foods met 48 to 64 per cent RDA. Consumption of milk and milk products, fruits, nuts and oilseeds, fats, oils, spices and codiments is almost nil.

From the nutrient intake data it can be seen that the intake of calories met 79 per cent RDA. The requirements of β-carotene and vitamin C met 20 and 50 per cent RDA, respectively. The intake of riboflavin met 64 per cent of RDA and niacin was nearly adequate. The intake of protein, calicum, iron, and thiamine was double that of the RDA.

Food and nutrient intake of the pre-school children

The food intake of pre-school children snows that the intake of cereal/ millets, and vegetables is in accordance with RDA but the consumption of pulse, oil seeds, green leafy vegetables is grossly inadequate as it meets only 24 and 11 per cent RDA, respectively. The consumption of roots, fruits, fats and oils is almost nil.

The requirement of not a single nutrient is fully met in the diets of the pre-school children. The intake of protein, iron and thiamine is met to the extent of 56 to 74 per cent. The intake of calcium and vitamin C met 16 per cent of RDA, β-carotene 10 per cent and riboflavin by approximately 30 per cent of RDA and niacin by 50 per cent.

NUTRIENTS AND EFFECT OF PROCESSING

The foods commonly consumed by the tribals, were analysed for proximate principles, minerals, vitamins and enzyme inhibitors. The results of the analysis are presented in Tables 4.16 to 4.24. The effect of processing of cereals/millets and legumes on vitamin content and protein digestibility (*in vitro*) was also studied and the results are presented in Tables 4.25 to 4.28.

Cereals and millets

From the figures presented in Tables 4.16 and 4.17 it is seen that no marked difference in proximate principles and vitamins is observed in

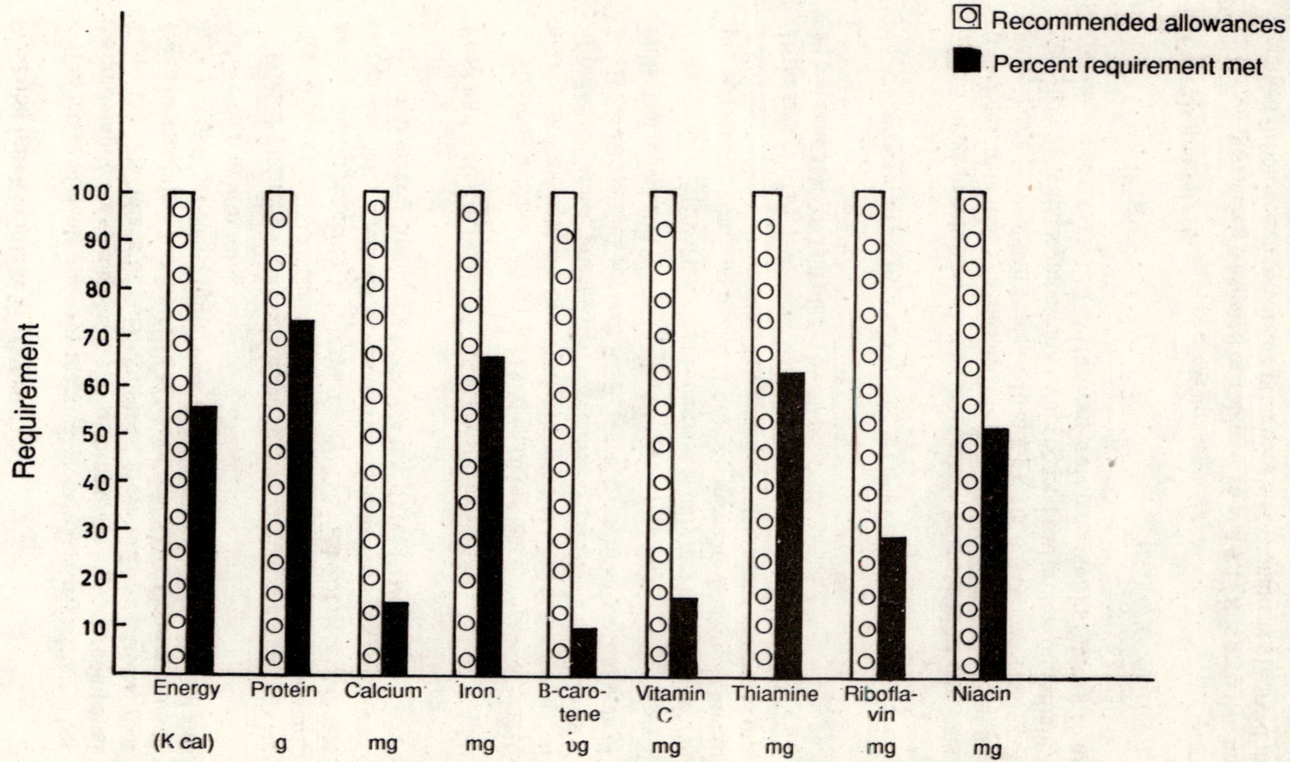

FIG. 8 . Percent of Nutrient requirements met by the Tribal Pre-school Children.

cereals and millets. The Calorie content of the cereal/millets range from 346 to 371 Kcal per 100 g, and protein ranges from 6.3 to 11.8 g per 100 g. Mineral content however, showed a marked variation. The values for calcium, phosophorus and iron range from 20 to 307 mg per 100 g, 118 to 797 mg per 100 g, and 5.2 to 19.3 mg per 100 g respectively. Calcium and iron content of *Punasa* and *Tella* varieties of ragi are higher.

Legumes

The nutrient composition of the legumes is presented in Tables 4.18 and 4.19.

Protein content of most of the legumes range from 20.2 to 23.8 g per cent excepting that of *Mucuna pruriens* which has a protein content of 27.3 g per cent. Calcium and iron content of the legumes range 20 to 351 mg per cent and 4.6 to 38.6 mg per cent, respectively. The lowest value for calcium is seen in *judumulu* (*Vigna* sp.) and the lowest iron content is seen in redgram grown in dry land. Horsegram has the high iron content of 38.6 mg per 200 g.

Tubers

The proximate composition, mineral and vitamin content of the wild tubers are presented in Tables 4.20 and 4.21.

The protein content of the tubers shows a range of 1.8 to 5.2 g per cent. The lowest value is recorded for *D. oppositifolia* and the highest for *D. hispida.* The fat content of *D. hispida* is 4.3 g per cent. Carbohydrate content of the tubers range from 15 to 27 g per cent. The energy value ranges from 72 Kcal to 134 Kcal. No marked differences are observed with respect to other nutrients.

The tubers and caryota palm pith are analysed for starch, *in vitro* starch digestibility and amylase inhibitor content. The results are presented in Table 38. The findings indicate that the total starch content of the raw tubers range from 11 to 21 per cent and that of caryota palm pith is 61 per cent. Total starch content of the food as per cent carbohydrate show a range of 75.7 to 86.9 per cent. The *in vitro* starch disgestibility (IVSD) analysed in raw tubers range from 8.7 to 11.5 per cent and caryota palm pith has an IVSD, 5.9 per cent. The amylase inhibitor units (AIU) of the tubers varies from 80 to 400 AIU and that of caryota palm pith is 712 AIU.

TABLE 4.16

Proximate composition of cereals and millets consumed by the tribals (per 100g edible portion)

Cereals/millets	*Particulars*	*Moisture (g)*	*Protein (g)*	*Fat (g)*	*Minerals (g)*	*Fibre (g)*	**Carbohydrate (g)*	*Energy kcal*
Bajra (*Pennisetum typhoideum*)	Local variety	9.5	8.4	3.1	1.7	1.2	76	366
	Hybrid variety (BJ 104)	10.2	10.0	3.6	1.6	1.4	73	364
Italian millet (*Setaria italica*)	Parboiled	9.8	11.8	3.1	1.1	0.2	74	371
	Raw	12.5	11.2	2.6	1.3	0.3	72	357
Jowar (*sorghum vulgare*)	White variety	13.4	8.4	2.9	1.9	0.3	73	352
	Red variety	14.8	7.0	2.9	1.6	0.3	73	346
Varagu (*Paspalum scrobiculatum*)	Parboiled	11.8	7.0	3.2	1.1	0.2	76	360
Sanwa (*Echinochloa frumentacea*)	Parboiled	10.5	10.9	1.2	1.3	0.3	76	358
Ragi (*Eleusine coracana*)	*Tella*	8.8	7.4	1.8	2.9	2.5	77	352
	Punasa	15.0	7.0	1.8	2.6	2.0	72	331
	Burada	10.5	7.0	1.4	2.3	2.1	77	347
Rice (*Oryza sativa*)	Raw	11.1	6.3	1.0	0.6	0.2	81	357
	Parboiled	11.5	6.5	0.8	0.9	0.2	80	354
	Red rice	8.5	6.3	0.7	1.2	0.3	83	364
Samai (*Panicum miliare*)	Parboiled	12.4	7.0	1.1	1.3	0.2	78	350

*By difference.

TABLE 4.17

Mineral and Vitamin content of cereals and millets consumed by tribals (per 100g edible portion)

Cereals/millets	*Particulars*	*Calcium (mg)*	*Phosphorus (mg)*	*Iron (mg)*	*Thiamine (mg)*	*Niacin (mg)*
Bajra	Local variety	27	797	6.5	0.30	3.4
(*Pennisetum typhoideum*)	Hybrid variety	20	714	7.2	0.31	3.5
Italian millet	Parboiled	20	460	8.7	0.31	2.3
(*Setaria italica*)	Raw	21	616	10.2	0.23	2.3
Jowar	White variety	28	161	5.2	0.23	2.2
(*Sorghum vulgare*)	Red variety	95	773	6.6	0.30	3.4
Varagu	Parboiled	22	161	5.8	0.34	3.4
(*Paspalum scrobiculatum*)						
Sanwa millet	Parboiled	20	544	8.6	0.34	2.2
(*Echinochloa frumentacea*)						
Ragi	*Tella*	302	656	19.3	0.40	1.2
(*Eleusine coracana*)	*Punasa*	307	479	18.8	0.31	1.0
	Burada	264	501	8.6	0.32	1.0
Rice	Raw	14	118	11.0	0.22	0.9
(*Oryza sativa*)	Parboiled	15	378	7.3	0.25	3.3
	Red rice	21	250	6.1	0.26	3.3
Samai (*Panicum miliare*)	Parboiled	21	390	8.8	0.31	2.1

TABLE 4.18
Proximate composition of legumes consumed by the tribals (per 100g edible portion)

Legumes	*Moisture (g)*	*Protein (g)*	*Fat (g)*	*Minerals (g)*	*Fibre (g)*	*Carbohydrate* (g)*	*Energy kcal*
Blackgram (*Phaseolus mungo*)	5.7	23.8	2.7	3.3	3.2	61	365
Cowpea (*Vigna catjang*)	7.4	22.1	0.9	3.9	-3.8	62	343
Field bean (dry) (*Dolichos lablab*)							
Black variety	7.5	20.3	1.4	3.2	4.4	63	345
White variety	8.4	20.3	2.4	3.4	2.4	63	355
Red variety	6.6	20.3	2.9	3.7	2.4	64	364
Judumulu (*Vigna* sp.)	10.7	22.0	2.1	3.4	1.1	61	350
Horsegram (*Dolichos biflorus*)							
Black variety	9.6	22.2	3.0	3.6	3.4	58	349
White variety	9.9	22.8	2.9	3.5	3.3	58	348
Redgram (*Cajanus cajan*)							
Dry land cultivated	7.8	20.3	2.7	3.5	5.8	60	345
Hill cultivated	4.7	20.3	2.6	3.5	5.0	64	359
Dukka chikkudu (*Mucuna pruriens*)	6.8	27.3	8.6	3.4	0.2	54	401

*By difference.

TABLE 4.19

Mineral and vitamin content of legumes consumed by the tribals (per 100g edible portion)

Legumes	*Calcium (mg)*	*Phosphorus (mg)*	*Iron (mg)*	*Thiamine (mg)*	*Riboflavin (mg)*	*Niacin (mg)*
Blackgram (*Phaseolus mungo*)	126	408	7.2	0.11	—	0.1
Cowpea (*Vigna catjang*)	304	345	13.1	0.12	—	0.1
Field bean (dry) (*Dolichos lablab*)						
Black variety	61	223	10.4	0.13	—	1.7
White variety	62	264	6.1	0.14	—	1.1
Red variety	78	355	11.8	0.23	—	2.5
Judumulu (*Vigna* sp.)	20	423	8.0	0.12	0.13	1.3
Horsegram (*Dolichos biflorus*)						
Black variety	263	515	38.6	0.31	—	3.5
White variety	351	448	37.5	0.22	—	3.0
Redgram (*Cajanus cajan*)						
Dry land cultivated	118	286	4.6	0.42	—	1.5
Hill cultivated	77	203	7.2	0.43	—	1.3
Dukka chikkudu (*Mucuna pruriens*)	30	346	8.8	0.13	0.10	1.6

—Not Estimated.

TABLE 4.20

Proximate composition of some wild tubers consumed by the tribals (per 100g edible portion)

Tubers	*Moisture (g)*	*Protein (g)*	*Fat (g)*	*Minerals (g)*	*Fibre (g)*	*Carbohydrate (g)*	*Energy (kcal)*
Arika tega (*Dioscorea oppositifolia*)	73	1.8	1.1	2.4	0.9	21	100
Chedu dumpa (*D. bulbifera*)	67	3.4	1.1	0.9	0.5	27	132
Pandimukku tega (*D. pentaphylla*)	79	2.8	0.7	3.2	2.0	15	72
Pulidumpa (*D. hispida*)	74	5.2	4.3	2.0	0.8	19	134

TABLE 4.21

Mineral and vitamin content in some wild tubers consumed by the tribals (per 100g edible portion)

Tubers	*Calcium (mg)*	*Phosphorus (mg)*	*Iron mg*	*Thiamine mg*	*Riboflavin mg*	*Niacin mg*
Arika tega (*Discorea Oppositifolia*)	45	53	4.7	0.04	0.02	0.10
Chedu dumpa (*D. Pentaphylla*)	56	175	6.4	0.04	0.02	0.06
Pandimukku tega (*D. bulbifera*)	139	177	7.2	0.02	0.02	0.10
Pulidumpa (*D. hispida*)	86	15	4.7	0.10	0.02	0.40

TABLE 4.22
***In vitro* digestibility of starch and amylase of starch and amylase inhibitor content in some tubers**

Tubes	**Total starch per cent*	*Total starch as per cent carbohydrate*	*Per cent in vitro starch digestibility*	*Amylase inhibitor activity AIU 100g*
Arika tega (D. Oppositifolia)	16.84	80.9	11.5	80
Chedu dumpa (D. bulbifera)	20.8	76.7	10.6	400
Pandimukku tega (D. pentaphylla)	11.43	78.8	8.7	240
Pulidumpa (D. hispida)	16.09	86.9	9.5	80
Caryota palm pith (caryota urens)	60.7	75.7	5.9	712

*On fresh weight basis.

Miscellaneous foods

Nutrient composition of the miscellaneous foods consumed by the tribals is presented in Tables 4.23 to 4.24. From the data (Table 4.23) it is seen that caryota palm pith is lower in protein value, being 1.8 g per cent and processed and dried bamboo shoot has higher protein content (29.69 g per cent). The cereal like grains rajkeera seeds (*Amaranthus Paniculatus)* and gingelly seed cake product has fat content of 7.2 g per cent. It is seen from Table 4.24, that calcium content of dried mushroom, dried bamboo shoot and caryota palm pith is negligible. The calcium content of gingelly seed cake product is 965 mg per cent. Iron content of miscellaneous foods range from 5.9 mg (black-gram crisps) to 92 mg per cent in mushroom (dried). Niacin content of the foods range from 0.03 to 2.3 mg per cent, bamboo shoots having low niacin and gingelly product with high niancin content.

The method of cooking of cereals and millets by tribals somewhat differs from that of non-tribals. An attempt therefore is made to study the effect of such processing on some important nutrients.

The effect of cereal and millet processing on thiamine and niacin content and protein digestibility (*in vitro*) in cereals/millets and legumes is presented in this section. The effect of boiling and fermentation on thiamine and niacin content of cereals and millets is presented in Table 4.25.

Effect of processing on vitamin content of cereals and millets

A loss of 75 to 100 per cent of thiamine and loss of 24 to 71 per cent of niacin is observed in the cereals/millets due to boiling and draining. Fermentation of ragi gruel increased the thiamine content by 50 per cent and niacin by 36 per cent. No increase in thiamine and niacin is observed in the cooked products kept over-night in water.

Effect of processing of IVPD of cereals, millets and pulses

The effect of processing on the IVPD of cereals, millets and pulses is presented in Tables 4.26 and 4.27 respectively. The IVPD of cereals/millets before and after cooking ranges from 43 to 97 per cent and 19 to 85 per cent respectively. The results indicate reduction of 9 to 24 per cent in IVPD of cereals/millets due to boiling. The loss in IVPD is less

TABLE 4.23

Proximate composition of miscellaneous Foods consumed by the tribes (per 100g edible portion)

Miscellaneous foods	*Moisture (g)*	*Protein (g)*	*Fat (g)*	*Mineral (g)*	*Fibre (g)*	*Carbohydrate* (g)*	*Energy kcal*
Bamboo shoots processed and dried (*Bambusa arundinacea*)	11.6	29.6	0.4	8.5	6.9	43	294
Mushroom (dried) (*Agaricus sp.*)	10.5	27.6	2.9	9.5	9.2	71	298
Caryota palm pith (Zillugu pindi) (*Caryota urens*)	10.1	1.8	0.4	2.0	5.5	80	332'
Rajkeera seeds (*Amaranthus paniculatus*)	3.2	16.8	7.2	2.7	1.0	69	407
Blackgram crisps (*Phaseolus mungo*	17.2	18.3	0.4	2.0	0.1	62	325
Pindi vadialu (made of gingelly seed cake) (*Sesamum indicum*)	40.8	14.3	7.3	10.2	2.8	25	222

*By difference.

TABLE 4.24

Mineral and vitamin content of miscellaneous foods consumed by the tribes (per 100g edible portion)

Miscellaneous foods	*Calcium (mg)*	*Phosphorus (mg)*	*Iron (mg)*	*Thiamine (mg)*	*Riboflavin (mg)*	*Niacin (mg)*
Bamboo shoots processed and dried (*Bambusa arundinacea*)	3	1049	22	0.05	0.01	0.03
Mushroom (dried) (*Agaricus sp.*)	5	1193	92	0.31	0.20	0.70
Caryota palm pith (Zillugu pindi) (*Caryota urens*)	0	72	51.7	0.12	0.02	0.02
Rajkeera crisps (*Amaranthus paniculatus*)	116	419	48.9	0.04	0.40	2.00
Blackgram crisps (*Phaseolus mungo*)	84	570	5.9	0.13	—	1.80
Pindi vadialu (Made of gingelly seed cake) (*Sesamum indicum*)	965	1598	38.4	0.40	—	2.30

—Not Estimated.

TABLE 4.25

Effect of processing on thiamine and niacin content of the cereals and millets consumed by the tribes

Cereals and millets	Vitamin content (mg/100 g)									
	Before cooking		After cooking		Per cent loss/gain		Product with conjee kept over night		Per cent loss/gain	
	Thiamine	Niacin	Thiamine	Niacin	Thiamine	Niacin	Thiamine	Niacin	Thiamine	Niacin
Rice	0.15	1.2	0	0.6	–100	±50	0.25	0.5	+66	–56
Combination of Bajra and rice	0.22	2.1	0.01	0.6	–95	–75	0.30	0.9	+36	–57
Combination of *Korra* and rice	0.41	2.0	0.02	1.4	–95	–30	0.35	1.4	-14	–30
Korra rice	0.33	1.5	0.01	0.4	–97	–40	0.25	1.1	-24	–20
Korra rice (Parboiled)	0.35	2.6	0.05	1.9	–86	–27	0.26	2.2	-25	–15
Ooda rice (Parboiled)	0.40	1.5	0.10	0.9	–75	–40	0.20	0.7	-50	–53
Jowar rice	0.21	2.5	0.02	0.9	–90	–64	0.30	2.2	+43	–12
Ragi gruel (fermented)	0.40	1.1	0.60	1.5	+50	+36	–	–	–	–
Bajra gruel (unfermented)	0.30	3.7	0.05	2.8	–83	–24	–	–	–	–

TABLE 4.26

Effect of processing on *in vitro* protein digestibility of the cereals and millets

Cereal and millet preparations	*% IVPD*		*Per cent loss*
	Before cooking	*After cooking*	
Rice	97	85	–12
Combination of Bajra and rice	97	75	–22
Combination of *korra* and rice	87	78	–9
Korra rice (unparboiled)	78	67	–11
Korra rice (parboiled)	77	61	–16
Ooda rice (parboiled)	73	59	–14
Jowar rice	81	71	–10
Ragi gruel (fermented)	43	19	–24
Bajra gruel (unfermented)	96	76	–20

TABLE 4.27
Effect of processing on *in vitro* protein digestibility of the legumes

Legume	*% IVPD*		*Per cent*
	Before cooking	*After cooking*	*improvement*
Cowpea (green)	69	88	19
(*Vigna catjang*)			
Field bean (dry)			
(*Dolichos lablab*)			
Black	40	70	30
White	72	98	26
Red	67	99	32
Judumulu	65	80	15
(*Vigna* sp.)			
Horsegram			
(*Dolichos lablab*)			
White	65	80	15
Black	62	83	21
Redgram			
(*Cajanus Cajan*)			
Dryland Cultivated	71	100	29
Hill Cultivated	70	99	29
Dukka chikkud (dehusked)	40	70	30
(*Mucuna Pruriens*)			

TABLE 4.28
Effect of processing on the trypsin inhibitor content of the legumes

Legume	*TIU/ml of extract*		*Per cent*
	Before cooking	*After cooking*	*loss of TIU*
Cowpea (green) (*Vigna catjang*)	51	11	78.0
Field bean dry (*Dolichos lablab*)			
Black variety	50	14	72.0
White variety	52	9	82.7
Red variety	53	7	86.8
Judumulu (*Vigna* sp.)	50	11	78.0
Horsegram (*Dolichos biflorus*)			
White variety	49	8	83.7
Black variety	50	10	80.0
Redgram (*Cajanus cajan*)			
Dryland Cultivated	49	8	83.7
Hill cultivated	51	8	84.3
Dukka Chikkudu (*Mucuna Pruriens*)	39	6	84.6

(9 per cent) in *korra* and rice combination product, and the loss is maximum (24 per cent) in ragi gruel.

The IVPD of unprocessed pulses ranges from 40 to 73 per cent and processed legumes range from 70 to 100 per cent indicating an appreciable increase in IVPD due to boiling of legumes. Maximum increase (30 per cent) in IVPD was seen in field bean black variety, and *dukka chikkudu* (dehusked), and least improvement in the digestibility was observed on boiling of the legumes judumulu and horsegram white variety.

Effect of processing on trypsin in inhibitor content of legume

Effect on processing on the trypsin inhibitor content of the legumes is presented in Table 44. All the varieties of legumes have tryps in-inhibitor. However, most of it is destroyed in the cooking process. The results indicate 72 to 87 per cent of the destruction of the inhibitor due to boiling. Maximum destruction of trypsin inhibitor content is observed in field bean, red variety, and minimum destruction with field bean, black, variety.

CHAPTER 5

DISCUSSIONS

The male to female sex ratio of the tribal population studied is 1000/1032 and is almost similar to that of total population of Vizianagaram district. (Bureau of Economics and Statistics, 1981). But the ratio is somewhat higher when compared to that of 1981 Census of India (1000:935). Since sex ratio is the crucial indicator of women's health status and survival, the higher ratio observed in the present data indicate that the incidence of mortality among the tribal women is not very high.

DEMOGRAPHY AND SOCIO-ECONOMIC CONDITIONS

The size and growth of population has a strong bearing on the situation and on the process of human development. The dependency ratio of a population is a more complex but more useful parameter of economic condition of the population. The age group 15-59 years is an economically productive segment of the population on whom the other age groups are dependent. The dependency ratio is based on the fact that every member of a society is a consumer but that only some members are producers.

The total youth dependency ratio of the tribal group studied was found to be 26.5 per cent which is far less compared to figures of India (76 per cent) cited by Thompson and Lewis (1980), which means that the dependent population is much less in the tribal group. Dependency ratio will be higher if life expectancy is higher, family size is larger and infant mortality lower. Perhaps none of these three factors is true for the study group and consequently the dependency ratio is low. It is observed that while children below 14 years are 37 per cent and children below 6 years are 13 per cent in the present study group, the corresponding figures of India are 40 per cent and 17 per cent resepectively (Census of India, 1981; UNICEF, 1984) which are higher. These disparities indicate higher mortality rate among the children in the tribal population or low fertility rate in the tribals.

Family size

The average family size of the present group of tribals is 4.63 which is lower than that of 1981 average for India, 5.0 (India, 1981). It is seen that 58 per cent of the tribal families have an average family size of 4 to 5 and the same trend is observed in all the four tribes studied. The smaller family size is attributable to various socio-cultural factors like pre-marital relations, equal liberty between the sexes to divorce and re-marriage and the high incidence of STD *etc*. The tribals also have a considerable knowledge of medicinal herbs which they use as contraceptives. Therefore it is possible that they are aware of effective measures to control birth. Similar comment is made by Gore *et al*, (1977), and Ali (1978-79) in their studies on tribals in Indravati river basin and Orissa.

Occupation

Agriculture is the primary occupation of a majority of the tribal families and agricultural labour is the secondary occupation, indicating that the tribal economy is mainly based on agriculture and the allied labour. Gadaba tribe, however, is an exception, in that, majority of them is found to be non-agriculturists. They earn their living by stone-cutting or agriculture labour, depending on the season. It is learnt that their ancestors were basically agriculturists, but the lands were taken away by money-lenders when they failed to repay the debt. Another striking feature that emerges from Table 4.3 is that tribals engaged in government jobs form only a small percentage. They hold only menial jobs and are mostly employed as cooks and watchmen in ashram schools or in government offices. This reflects the low educational levels of the tribals. The per cent literates in tribals of Vizianagaram district is reported to be only 7.98 per cent (Bureau of Economics and Statistics, 1981-82). Though Government is taking intensive measures to educate the tribals, the per cent literacy in the tribals is still very low. Adult education classes must be available to the tribals living in interior villages.

Collection of forest produce formed a part of the economy with all the tribes studied, irrespective of whether they owned land or not. The forest produce available includes *adda* leaf and seeds (*Bauhinia Vahlii*), tamarind, mahuva flowers (*Bassia longifolia*) and marking nut (*Senecarpus anacardium*). Some are also of medicinal value like *Nux Vomica*, (*Strychnos nux-vomica*), *Patala garidi Rawulfia serpentina*, myrobalan *etc*. Studies on tribals from different parts of the country also indicated that agriculture and food gathering formed the main sustenance with majority of the tribals (Pingale, 1973; Sen Gupta 1980; Rao, 1971.; Roy and Rao 1962; Swaminathan *et al*, 1971; Rao and Satyanarayana, 1974; Bhowmik, 1971). However, no particular information is available on the economic contribution of the forest produce. Even in the present study it was difficult to gather correct information on income from forest produce.

Regarding sharing of work, both men and women are actively engaged in agriculture work and labour. However, preparation of land for cultivation is considered a man's job and women are generally involved in sowing and harvesting apart from the daily household chores like cooking, child rearing and maintenance of house.

Land and agricultural pattern

Agricultural practices in any region usually depend on the type of land available and irrigation potential. Tribals practise both *podu* and settled cultivation. Tribals living in hilly areas practise *podu* cultivation, and those living in plain areas practise settled cultivation. Wherever small streams pass through, they build bunds with stones and divert water to their fields and cultivate paddy. This is known as terrace cultivation. However, tribals in general prefer *podu* cultivation as it involves less work and no use of cattle. Moreover, cultivation of more number of crops is possible as compared to plain cultivation. Therefore, the recent concern of the government to persuade them to wean from *podu* cultivation may be successful only through proper incentives coupled with a practical approach to the problem. The tribals grow paddy and various major and minor millets, legume crops, oilseeds and also other cash crops like turmeric and tobacco. Vegetables like brinjal, beans, gourds, pumpkin are also grown both in fields and in the backyards of their houses. The diversity of the food crops cultivated by the tribals should be encouraged. However, considering the poor quality of their diets (Tables 4.12 to 4.15), cultivation and consumption of more of leafy vegetables like gogu, amaranth, tamarind, and drumstick leaves and root vegetables like carrots, beetroots, potato, sweet potato and fruits like amla, lime, guava, papaya, jack fruit, mango, orange, rich in β-carotene, vitamin C, calcium and iron should be encouraged.

In spite of the diverse staple food crops grown by the tribals, their ability to store for a less period (Table 4.6) indicates that the grain yields are low. Therefore, steps for increasing agricutural production by introducing better technology and supply of improved and high yielding varieties of seeds and fertilizers in time should be intensified. While encouraging cultivation of cash crops to improve their economy, care should be taken that it is not at the expense of staple food crops as it affects the quality and quantity of their diets.

Morbidity

From the morbidity records (Table 4.7) it is evident that scabies and dermatitis are the major health problems in the area followed by infection and infestation. The high incidence of skin diseases in the area reflect their poor personal and environmental hygiene. Among the diseases related to eye, 97 per cent of the cases are due to infection and ony 3 per cent are of nutritional origin. When compared to NNMB reports (1981) the incidence of xerosis and bitot spots in the tribals is less. The incidence of B-complex deficiency in the tribal population is 7 per cent whereas the average figure reported in the rural population of Andhra Pradesh is 13.65 per cent (NNMB,1981). Earlier studies on various tribal groups in the country also revealed that the incidence of scabies, infection, infestation, and malnutrition are rampant in the areas (Ali, 1978-79; NIN, 1963; 1969; and 1973; Pingale, 1973; Pratap *et al*, 1976; Sharma, 1979; Gore *et al*, 1977). Health is an obvious function of nutrition and in most of the underdeveloped areas in the world, food deficiencies arise in a hostile environment where poor personal and environmental hygiene, inadequate housing and lack of adequate potable water prevails. Therefore, added to malnutrition, there are multiple illnesses resulting from infection and parasites that sap to an even greater extent the health and well-being of the people. Though provision of medical facilities can cure, prevention is possible by health education. Since the effect of malnutrition and infections are synergestic, the combined efforts of both health and nutrition personnel is essential.

The impact of acculturation, that is changes in their mode of dressing too, might have adversely added to poor hygienic practices and this should not be overlooked. Covering their body with more clothes might have accentuated the problem of scabies, the personal hygiene remaining poor. Another contributory factor to poor hygiene is the long distance travelled by the woman to fetch water. This natrually leads to a practice of economising on use of water thus leading to poor hygiene. Smoking and consumption of alcohol might also add to the health problems.

It should be mentioned, however, that the general morbidity incidence data obtained from the PHC's in the blocks could give only an abstract of health problem in the area as majority of the tribals usually depend on native medicines and only serious cases are referred to the hospitals. Therefore, to get a clear picture of their health problems, a systematic epidemiological survey may prove to be quite useful.

Dietary pattern

The staple food of majority of the tribals is millets. Rice is also consumed though to a lesser extent than millets. Since millets grow in a wide range of soils and climates, as in semi-arid regions, their production and consumption might be popular with the tribals. Lack of irrigation facilities might have limited the production and use of paddy.

Tribals who depend mainly on daily wages buy mostly rice to aviod the tedious process of dehusking. However, considering the qualitative aspects, millets provide more protein, B-vitamins and minerals compared to rice and the use of millets could be encouraged. Processing of millets should be made easier by improved processing techniques that are within the reach of the tribals. If millets are made available in the fair price shops located in proximity, it also helps to promote and continue the practice of consumption of millets. It is evident from the diet survey that the bulk density of their diet is low as the staple grain is consumed mostly in gruel from. It is a traditional habit for the tribals to consume the millets in gruel form as they care more for volume of food which readily fills the stomach. This aspect needs the attention of nutritionists who are studying the tribal food habits.

Food fads and fallacies

As pointed out by Morose (1984), improper feeding practices adopted by the tribals and their lack of awareness on the importance of child health and nutrition cannot be isolated from the underlying cultural beliefs and practices. The tribals have the practice of feeding the new born with colostrum which is good and should be encouraged. However, children are weaned after one year and are directly put to an adult diet. Another striking factor that can be observed in Table 4.10 is that nearly 1/3 of Godabas suggested less than one year as age of weaning. The occupational differences (Table 4.3) may play a role in their practices. The Gadabas are engaged mostly in non-agricultural operations and so they may not find time to breast feed the infants leisurely or their milk output may be low whch may in turn result in early weaning and the poor nutritional status of the children. Since late and improper weaning affects child nutrition and growth, mothers of tribal communities should be given nutrition education on importance of proper supplementary feeding and preparation of foods for children.

Some of the traditional food practices of the triabls however are found good. The practices of parboiling the newly harvested millets—*sama*, *ooda*, *korra* and paddy seem to have been evolved by the tribals as an effective measure to improve the taste and cooking quality of the grains, as is indicated from their belief that parboiling makes dehusking easier, and the parboiled rice tastes better and less sticky after cooking. However, the traditional method of parboiling (boiling the grains for an hour) followed by the tribals may be modified and made less tedious with appropriate technology.

Some of the cooking practices of the tribals like cooking rice and millets together, korra and green leafy vegetables together, are good in terms of their complementary nutritional value.

Tribals prefer sour taste to sweet taste. Some food beliefs of tribals are irrational such as avoiding various foods during lactation. Confirmation may be needed with regard to galactogogues and foods attributed to have specific medicinal importance. Most of their beliefs are centered around taste, processing, cooking quality, availability, sustenance *etc*., and so nutrition education can help to reform some of their incorrect attitudes.

FOOD INTAKE OF WOMEN

In any community it can be presumed that if requirements of vulnerable segments are met, the requirements of others too would have been met. The food and nutrient intake is discussed with refernce to Recommended Dietary Allowances (RDA) for Indians (ICMR, 1981) and with average consumption of food (g/cu/day) in rural areas of Andhra Pradesh (NNMB, 1981). It is also compared with dietary studies available on various tribal families.

Cereals, millets, pulses and oilseeds

The intake of cereals by the tribal women is found to be satisfactory as compared with the RDA wheareas the intake of pulses/oilseeds met 55 per cent RDA. The important pulse crops grown by the tribals are redgram *judumulu*, horsegram oilseed crops are groundnut, gingelly and niger seeds. Though various pulses and oilseeds are grown by the tribals, most of it is exchanged by the tribals to purchase staple food items or to meet any incidental expenses which results in inadequate intake of pulses. However, tribals are found to purchase and consume blackgram crisps and a product of gingelly seed cake very frequently. Both the products are consumed in combination with a vegetable or dry fish. This implies that tribal women are not aware of preparing products with longer shelf life. Secondly, they are exploited by the vendors who purchase pulses from them.

Intake of cereals to pulses is found to be in the ratio of 17:1, as against the ideal ratio of 7:1 recommendend by ICMR (1981). In spite of production of pulses, consumption is low because the tribals have a ready market for it. In addition, tribals are exploited by businessmen who try to procure pulses from the tribals at low prices. Since pulses are one of the easily saleable commodities, tribals are deprived of it. Therefore, it seems that it is not awareness or availability that limits pulse consumption but their poor economic condition. Therefore steps in increasing the production of pulses, proper organisation of marketing facilities coupled with nutrition education are necessary to increase the consumption of pulses and economic conditions. The same holds good in the production of oilseeds too.

In cereal-pulse based diet, the first limiting amino acid is not lysine but the sulphur containing aminoacids (Srikantia, 1984). Gingelly seeds being rich in methonine, is a good supplement to cereal-pulse based diets. However the gingelly product consumed by the tribals is prepared from whole gingelly seed cake and the oil content of the product is found to be high (7 g per 100 g) (Table 4.23). Therefore, the health implication in terms of the inadequate and improper oil extraction procedures with country '*ghani*' should not be overlooked as the high oil content of it may affect the shelf-life of the product. It might be quite possible that the addition of spices in the preparation of the product too may mask off flavours due to rancidity. Therefore, an alternative or improved product of gingelly seed cake may help to improve the quality of the diet.

Vegetables

Consumption of vegetables by the women is found to be 50 per cent higher than RDA. Compared to the intake of tribals of East Godavari district (51 g) (Pushpamma *et al*, 1983) and of rural population (47 g) of Andhra Pradesh, (NNMB, 1981), consumption of vegetables by the tribals is much higher. Vegetables come next to staple grains in consumption, as cultivation of vegetables is the common practice with almost all the tribals. Vegetables commonly grown by them are yellow pumpkin, legume vegetables, gourds and beans. Availability of land and/or tradition might have encouraged them to grow these vegetables. Production and consumption of variety of nutritious vegetables should be encouraged as they provide some important nutrients besides adding variety to the diet.

At the time of the collection of general information during September-October 1982, tender bamboo shoots were available aplenty. It was observed that the tribals consume these shoots almost regularly. However, this was not so with the tribals of the Pachipenta block as the bamboo forests were reported to have died and the shoots are not available. This shows that the tribals do not have particular choice for foods but are accustomed to eat whatever is available and edible in nature at any given time.

The intake of green leafy vegetables met 58 per cent RDA and purchasing leafy vegetables is a rare phenomenon in the tribals. Compared to rural population in Andhra Pradesh (NNMB, 1981) consumption of green leafy vegetables by the tribals is five times higher. The consumption of leafy vegetables by tribals of East Godavari district (Pushpamma *et al*, 1983) is reported to be negligible. However, family dietary studies conducted on Chenchus of Andhra Pradesh in summer and rainy seasons reported a higher intake (240 g) of green leafy vegetables (Pratap, 1973) which is quite high compared to that of the intake by the tribals under study. Tradition and availability may influence consumption. Tender bamboo shoots available from August through October are abundantly used by the tribals.

Consumption of root vegetables met only 45 per cent RDA and is almost similar to that of rural population (NNMB, 1981). Other studies on tribals of East Godavari district (Pushpamma *et al*, 1983) reported an intake of 19g and is almost similar to the findings in the present study. In the present study onions form the main root vegetable and are purchased from shandy. The tribals do cultivate roots like yam, colocasia in their backyards. Though the tribals are familiar with the wild roots available in the forests, their inclusion in the diets is said to be on the decline. It is perhaps due to the strenuous and elaborate process of searching, digging and processing involved prior to their consumption. Perhaps it is also likely that the chronic calorie deficiency in their diets has resulted in withdrawal of high energy activities. They may also not find time for procuring and processing wild roots, being engaged in labour work closer to their homes. However, considering the energy value of the root vegetables, cultivation of roots like yam, sweet potato, potato, *etc*., need to be encouraged. In general,apart from the production and consumption of root vegetables, other vegetables of high nutritive value like pumpkin, drumstick, tomatoes and green leafy vegetables which are good source of calcium, iron, β-carotene, vitamin C and B-vitamins should be encouraged. Since most of the tribals are found to be dependent on home gardens for their vegetable needs, proper crop planning in the space available, and supply of high yielding variety seeds, fertilizers and other related inputs will not only encourage production and consumption of vegetables of nutritive importance, but also help improve their economy. Tribals are found to be ignorant of the use of some of the foods like tamarind leaves, mint, coriander leaves *etc*, in their diets. Nutrition education is therefore helpful in familiarising and encouraging production and use of such food which also provide quality to their dietaries.

Flesh foods

The consumption of flesh foods met only 64 per cent RDA. The average intake of fish and other flesh foods in the diets of rural population and of the tribals of East Godavari District reported an intake of 13g to 28g (NNMB, 1981; Pushpamma *et al*, 1983), and is almost similar to that of the present study. However, it should be noted that tribals usually consume flesh foods once or twice a week. The usual meal pattern is very simple (Table 4.10). The two major source of flesh foods in the diets of the tribals are cattle meat and dryfish and are frequently purchased from shandy. Cattle meat is purchased in quantity of 500 to 1000g and is consumed on the same day by the family. Dry fish however is used in small quantities (50-80g) for flavouring, cooked either in combination with some vegetables or blackgram crisps. Though rearing of domestic animals like cattle, pig, poultry *etc*, is common with the tribals, they do not sacrifice domesticated animals for meat purposes except on special occasions like marriages, festivals *etc*. Though poultry rearing is a common practice among the tribals, consumption of eggs is negligible. Eggs are used for hatching purposes so as to make money with chicken. Since rearing of domesticated animals is a traditional practice, what is required is that they need to be taught rearing of small animals like rabbits, pigs, birds, chicks, *etc*., so that consumption of meat can be made frequent. Provision of adequate storage and marketing facilities coupled with proper training will help them to rear more animals. Tribals seem to relish pig meat and since it is economical too, piggery should be encouraged. Artificial ponds should be encouraged by diverting the stream water for fish production.

Miscellaneous foods

The consumption of sugar and jaggery, fats and oils, spices and condiments is negligible in their daily diets and are used only on special occasions. The over-all improvement in their socio-economic conditions, provision of facilities for the production, coupled with nutrition education will bring an improvetment in their diets both qualitatively and quantitatively. One striking feature in the food intake of the tribals is an observation that the consumption of milk by these people is nil in spite of the fact they have with them many cows, buffaloes and goats. This is beacuse they use these animals mainly for cultivation and for sacrifices on special occasions, and milking is considered, a sin.

NUTRIENTS IN THE DIET OF WOMEN

Calories and proteins

The calorie content of the diets of the women met 88 per cent of RDA. When compared with the diets of rural population of Andhra Pradesh (2390 Kcal) the intake is less (NNMB, 1981). The requirement of protein met RDA but is slightly low when compared with that of rurual population of Andhra Pradesh (NNMB, 1981). Various studies on tribals in India reported a wide range in the intake of calories from 1600 to 2542 Kcal and protein 45g to 63g (Pingale, 1973; Sen Gupta, 1980; Sharma, 1979; Gore *et al*, 1977; Sharma, 1977; Pushpamma *et al*, 1983; Pratap, 1973).

The calorie gap observed in the present study may be mainly due to the low calorie density of their diets, which are largely in the form of gruel and also due to the use of negligible amount of fat in their diets.

However, the tribals being habituated to take 2 to 8 litres of millet beer daily, the contribution of calories from it should also be taken into account. Taking into consideration the alcohol content in the millet beer to be 5.2 per cent (Sen Gupta, 1960) the calorie deficit of 600-700 Kcal as seen in their diets is made good by the consumption of beer. However, its adverse effects on health and nutrition, especially on B vitamin should not be overlooked.

The protein in the present study is mostly derived from cereals/millets and gingelly seed cake. In the mixed cereal diet of Andhra Pradesh, tryptophan is reported to be the first limiting amino acid followed by isoleucine and sulphur amino acids and not lysine (Devadas and Murthy, 1977). Considering the complementary role of gingelly seed the protein quality of their diets is fairly good.

Calcium and Iron

Calcium and iron content of their diets are satisfactory. The intake of iron is double compared to rural and other tribals. (NNMB, 1981; Pingale, 1973; Sen Gupta, 1980; Pushpamma *et al*, 1983). However, some studies on Koyas of Orissa and Chenchus of Andhra Pradesh reported an intake of calcium as high as 830 mg to 1.2 g and iron 48 to 63 mg (Pratap 1973; Sharma, 1979). Seasonal availablity, tradition and agronomic conditions influence the intake.

The requirement of minerals in their diets is mainly derived from cereals/millets, gingelly seed cake and green leafy vegetables. The low intake of calcium by the women of the two tribes Gadaba amd Kondadora (Table 4.13) might be attributed to the low intake of green leafy vegetables. The availability of calcium from the whole gingelly seed cake is however questionable, as whole gingelly seeds, being high in oxalates form an insoluble calcium oxalate and render calcium unavailable to the body. The incidence of anaemia in these tribals in spite of the intake of iron in significant amount may be due to low availability of iron in these foods or due to the environmental conditions or high infestation in these areas.

β-carotene

The requirement of β-carotene met only 50 per cent RDA. Similar situation is reported in rural population of Andhra Pradesh too (NNMB, 1981). Other studies on tribals of Central India, Orissa, East Godavari district and some tribes of Andhra Pradesh reported an average intake of 344 to 613 μg of β-carotene (Pingale, 1973; Sen Gupta, 1980; Pushpamma *et al*, 1983; Pratap, 1973) and is almost equal to the intake by the women in the present study. Significant difference between the tribes of Bhadragiri and Pachipenta blocks may be attributed to variations in the intake of green leafy vegetables (Table 4.12). The wide gap in β-carotene in their diets is of great concern as it may subsequently affect the growth of the children. The morbidity data on the diseases related to eye (Table 4.7) also indicates the presence of bitot spots, night blindness and xerosis in the community. Therefore, production and consumption of β-carotene rich foods of vegetable origin like green leafy vegetables, fruits like mango, papaya, jack furit *etc*., should be encouraged through proper motivation and nutrition education.

Vitamin C

In spite of living in close proximity to nature, the intake of vitamin C by the tribal women is only half of RDA. Compared to rural population (NNMB, 1981) the intake of vitamin C by the tribal women is much less. Low intake of vitamin C by tribals, in different parts of India is reported (Pingale, 1973; Sen Gupta, 1980; Pushpamma *et al*, 1983). Considering the high rate of infections in the tribals of present study (Tables 4.7 and 4.8) and the preventive role of vitamin C, cultivation and consumption of vitamin C rich foods like berries, lime, guava, oranges amla and green leafy vegetables should be encouraged as it will increase their intake of vitamin C.

B-complex vitamins

The intake of thiamine and niacin are adequately met whereas the intake of riboflavin met only 64 per cent RDA. Similar trend was reported in the diets of rural and other tribal population of India (NNMB, 1981; Pingale, 1973; Sen Gupta, 1980; Pushpamma *et al*, 1983). Millets and vegetables formed the major source of thiamine and niacin. However, the morbidity data indicates that B-complex deficiency is one of the major nutritional problem in the area. The consumption of alcohol may be a risk as well as a contributory factor in this regard. Inadequate consumption of foods rich in riboflavin like milk, eggs and flesh foods, is perhaps the reason for the wide gap between intake and requirement of riboflavin. Although milch cattle are available, cultural stigma prevents them from consuming milk. It is learnt from the block level officials during the survey period that distribution of milch animals to the tribals did not yield any satisfactory results as the buffaloes were either used for agricultural purposes or killed for meat. It may take some time to persuade them to the habit of consuming milk, as cultural stigma is the major inhibiting factor. However it is important to convince the tribals to rear milch animals so that the consumption of milk by the family improves not only the quality of their diets but also betters their economy.

NUTRIENT INTAKE OF PRE-SCHOOL CHILDREN

The intake of cereals by the children is just adequate and consumption of pulses and green leafy vegetables is 50 per cent higher than RDA. Milk and milk products, fruits, flesh foods, fats and oils, sugar and jaggery are almost nil in their daily diets (Table4.14). This is becuase children are directly weaned to an adult diet which consists mainly of cereals and vegetables. The mean food intake of cereals, pulses and vegetables of tribal pre-school children in Andhra Pradesh is reported to be 167g, 30g and 19g, (Pratap *et al*, 1976) respectively. In rural set up, the bulk of the diet is cereals and pulses, with a little quantity of vegetable (NNMB, 1981), because vegetables are more expensive. Perhaps, the foods included with cereals depend upon the cost and availability.

No nutrient is adequately met in the diet of pre-schoolers. The intake of energy met only half RDA and that of protein, iron, thiamine and niacin met 50 to 74 per cent RDA. Their diets are grossly inadequate in calcium, β-carotene ascorbic acid and riboflavin. Similar findings were reported by earlier investigators (Rao and Satyanarayana, 1974; Rao *et al*, 1973; Pratap *et al*, 1976; Subha Rani, 1984; Gopaladas, *et al*. 1983; Horner *et al*, 1981). The dietary situation of non-tribal pre-school children in India too seemed to be of no exception. A dietary study in the five regions of India covering 3000 pre-school children showed that the calorie deficit was 30 to 40 per cent of RDA and the diets were reported to be lacking in riboflavin, ascorbic acid, vitamin A and calcium (Bailur, 1971).

The fact that even in the same community, diets of pre-school children are much deficient in all nutrients compared to women, shows that infant feeding practices and intra-family distribution of available food requires immediate attention.

Energy gap in the diets of pre-school children in the present study is attributed to low intake of calories due to the consumption of gruel type products and also due to failure of including foods of concentrated forms of energy like jaggery, sugar, oil, and roots in their diets. The gap in protein might also be due to non-inclusion of pulses, oilseeds and milk in the diets of children. The deficiencies of β-carotene, calcium, iron, vitamin C (Table 4.14) might be due to inadequate inclusion of milk, vegetables and fruits in their diets.

Clinical studies available on some Indian tribals and rural pre-school children of Andhra Pradesh showed that nearly 30 to 48 per cent of the children were suffering with varying degrees of protein calorie malnutrition (Gore *et al*, 1977; Gupta and Bhandare, 1972; NNMB, 1981).

The demographic data indicate that the per cent pre-school children population in the present study, is less compared to all India figures and it may reflect high incidence of mortality in this group. As also indicated by UNICEF (1984) and Gopalan (1979) various factors like late weaning, poor infant feeding practices, high incidence of infection and infestation in the area might have contributed to the poor dietary situation of the children. The situation poses a challenge to the nutritionists and health administrators. Since a child's diet can only be improved by overall improvement in the diet of the entire family, mothers shoud be given nutrition. Establishment of child care centres to look after the children, when parents are away at work and availabiltiy and proper use of health care facilities by the vulnerable section of the tribal population, setting up mobile health services so as to reach the interior areas, is the immediate need to improve the health situation of the tribals. It will take long time to bridge the gap if one waits till the mothers learn and implement the principles to improve the diets. Hence. immediate need is to initiate well organised supplementary feeding programmes for the pre-school children with simultaneous nutrition education programmes for the youth and mothers.

NUTRIENT COMPOSITION AND EFFECT OF PROCESSING

Cereals and millets

Bajra, jowar, ragi and rice are the staple grains consumed by the tribals. The nutrient compositon of foods grown in the area are compared with some of the improved and hybrid varieties obtained from agricultural and millet research stations in Andhra Pradesh. The interphase between agriculture and nutrition requires a considerable practical improtance in improving the nutrition and well-being of any community.

Bajra. : Tribals grow a hybird variety of bajra, Bajra-104 and also a traditional variety. As compared to the protein content of the hybrid varieties (12 to 15g per 100g) released from agricultural and millet research stations the two bajra varieties grown by the tribals have less protein content (Table 45). Hence, the high protein varieties may be encouraged in the tribal area. The traditional variety of bajra grown by the tribals has comparatively high niacin content to other bajra varieties reproted. The variety *visakhi* grown in Vizianagram district had high iron content (16 mg per cent). The acceptance of the new varieties greatly depend on various factors.

Jowar : The tribals cultivate white and red vareities of local jowar and no hybird vareity is grown by them. The white vareity, however, is preferred over the red vareity. The two varieties of jowar contained 8.4g g and 7.0 g, per cent protein. But the varieties released/grown in Andhra Pradesh had higher protein content (11.4 to 14.2 g). The preference for white variety is mainly based on the cooking characteristics of the grain. Since the tribals are habituated to eat whole jowar (dehusked) form and not as gruel or *roti* form, the grain that withstands to pounding without becoming powdery during dehulling process is mostly preferred. Yellow vareity is said to become powdery during dehulling process and hence was not preferred. Therefore, in introducing any new varieties in the tribal areas, consideration to the grain characteristics, that fit into local food preparation is essential.

Ragi: The ragi varieties grown by the tribals are *punasa*, *tella* and *burada*. Both protein and calcium content of varieties grown by tribals is less compared to varieties released by millet research station located in the same district. It is unfortunate that they were not motivated to grow improved varieties.

The iron content of the two ragi varieties grown by tribals is higher (19 mg per 200 g) compared to the other varieties grown in Andhra Pradesh. However, VR—550 obtained from research station Vizianagaram, is reported to have an iron content of 42.8 mg per 100g. Deosthale *et al*, (1970) reported 17.6 mg per cent in VR-7 ragi variety. From these observations it is presumed that the ragi varieties cultivated by tribals are fairly rich in iron content.

Table 5.1

Comparsion of nutrients of bajra varieties of the present study with hybrid varieties (per 100g)

Source from which samples obtained	*Variety*	*Protein g*	*Iron mg*	*Calcium mg*	*Thiamine mg*	*Niacin mg*	*Reference*
Present investigation	Local	8.4	6.5	27.0	0.30	3.4	
	Hybrid BJ 104	10.0	7.2	20.0	0.31	3.5	
Millet Research Stn. VZM (Hybrid varieties)	Bajra visakhi composite	12.9	16.2	105.8	-	1.4	*NRC,1980-85 (unpublished)
	Bajra VBS-3	14.5	7.6	96.2	-	1.5	
	Bajra VBS-4	12.1	2.9	101.1	-	1.2	
Coimbatore (Hybrid varieties)	MP 75, 78, 79, 31, 35, 51, 63, 104	13-13.8	-	-	-	-	+AICRP, 1980—85 (unpublished)
	APMR ROB, MP 47 MP 36; MP 61	15	-	-	-	-	

Ref: *Nutrition Research Cell, College of Home Science, APAU, Hyderabad,
+All India Co-ordinated Research Project, College of Home Science, APAU, Hyderabad.

TABLE 5.2

Comparison of nutrients of the jowar varieties of the present study with improved varieties (per 100 g)

Source from which samples obtained	*Variety g*	*Protein mg*	*Iron mg*	*Thiamine mg*	*Niacin mg*		*Reference*
Present study	White	8.4	6.5	27.0	0.30	3.4	
	Red	7.0	7.2	20.2	0.31	3.5	
All over India	CSH-1 and CSH-9	12.8	4.1	12.7	0.30	.27	AICRP, 1980-85
	CSH-5 and CSH-6	14.2	to	to	to	to	(unpublished)
	CSH-88	13.6	5.5	22.1	0.39	3.5	
Andhra Pradesh	White	11.4					AICRP, 1980-85
	Yellow	11.6					(unpublished)
	Red variety	14.0					

AICRP: Data of All India Co-ordinated Project, College of Home Science, APAU, Hyderabad.

Rice: The rice varieties grown by the tribals have less protein (7g per 100g) as compared to the protein content of some of the varieties RGL 1282; MTU 5195, 6024, 4569 and IRI 3525 (8g, 8.8g per 100g) released from agricultural research stations Amudalavalasa and Maruteru located in the adjoining disticts. Among the 30 varieties, collected from three regions of Andhra Pradesh (AICRP, 1980-85) three varieties namely Molakolukulu, Singh Bhavani, and IR—20 were reported to have higher protein content, the values being 9.8g,10.5g and 11.4g per cent, respectively. This shows, improved varieties have not been introduced in tribal area.

The mineral and vitamin content of the millet and rice varieties grown by the tribals are found to be slightly higher as compared to other varieties (Tables 4.28-5.2). Doggett (1984) had pointed out that the fertility of the soil and irrigation facilities available contribute to the differences in the nutrient composition of the same variety grown in different localities. Therefore, it would not be easy to predict whether the variety yields the same results when grown in other parts. However, the high yielding variety may be tried in tribal areas to improve the economy and yield which will be reflected in higher consumption in the long run.

Legumes : The protein content of the legumes cultivated by the tribals ranged from 20g to 27g/100g. The protein content is lower for redgram, higher for Mucuna pruriens (Table 4.18). Compared with the values reported (Table 2.8). Legume varieties grown by the tribals are in no way inferior to the varieties grown in various parts of the country.

The mineral content of the legumes analysed was found to be higher compared to the values reported in literature. Among the legumes studied, the iron content of horsegram is found to be quite high (38mg per cent) as compared with the value reported by Gopalan *et al* (1980). However, Kadwe *et al* (1974) reported a higher range of iron content (32-60 mg/ 100 g) in K-33, D-40-1 and D-1-8 varieties of horsegram grown in Marathwada region of Maharashtra. Climatic factors especially rainfall and temperature, soil and the kind of plant might influence the mineral composition as pointed by Beeson and Matrone, 1976; Kadwe *et al*, 1974; Becker, 1976. It could also be due to genetic factors.

One of the uncommon legumes namely *Judumulu* (*vigna* sp.) grown by the tribals has a protein content of 22 per cent which is well comparable with other legumes. *Dukka chikkudu* (*Mucuna pruriens*) another uncommon legume grown by the tribals is said to be toxic and needs a special

TABLE 5.3

Comparison of nutrients of ragi varieties of the present study with some other varieties (per 100g)

Source from which samples obtained	*Variety*	*Protein g*	*Iron mg*	*Calcium mg*	*Thiamine mg*	*Niacine mg*	*Reference*
Present study	*Tella*	7.48	19.3	302	0.40	1.20	
	Punasa	7.00	18.8	307	0.31	1.00	
	Burada	7.00	8.6	264	0.32	1.00	
Millet Research Station, Vizayanagram, Andhra Pradesh	VR250-6	10.48	9.52	442	—	0.75	NRC, 1980-85 (unpublished)
	VR 415	11.28	9.52	415	—	0.60	
	AKP-2	12.09	7.14	529	—	0.25	
	VR-520	12.09	5.95	513	—	0.35	
	VR-10.68	10.88	4.80	501	—	0.40	
	VR-550	9.21	42.84	513	—	0.43	
Agricultural Research Station, Peddapuram, Andhra Pradesh	Ragi-Godavari	9.18	6.00	509	—	0.60	NRC, 1980-85 (unpublished)
	Ragi-PR 1103	10.93	4.75	481	—	0.44	
	PR 230	11.37	8.25	501	—	0.55	
	PR 1091	12.25	8.25	601	—	0.45	
	PR 1044	14.43	4.75	561	—	0.43	
	PR 177	11.37	6.00	509	—	0.60	

NRC : Nutrition Research Cell, College of Home Science, APAU, Hyderabad.

TABLE 5.4

Comparison of nutrients of rice varieties of the present study with other varieties (per 100g)

Source from which samples obtained	*Variety*	*Protein g (Nx6.25)*	*Iron mg*	*Calcium mg*	*Thiamine mg*	*Niacin*	*Reference*
Present study	Local raw (hand-pounded)	6.99	12.2	14.99	0.22	2.1	
	Parboiled hand-pounded	7.24	8.13	16.16	0.28	3.7	
	Red Rice	6.84	6.61	23.0	0.21	3.6	
Agricultural Research station, Amudalavalasa (Srikakulam Dist, Andhra Pradesh)	RGL 1282	8.16	6.0	Nil	0.24	3.5	* NRC, 1980—85 (unpublished)
	Other varieties	5.60 to 7.90	2.67 to 3.67	Nil	0.19 to 0.32	2.4 to 2.5	
Agricultural Research Station, Maruteru West Godavari Andhra Pradesh	MTU 5195	8.51	0.4	—	—	—	*NRC, 1980—85 (unpublished)
	MTU6024	8.19	1.5	—	—	—	
	MTU 4569 and IRI 3525	8.80	0.9	—	—	—	
All over India	30 varieties	8.10 to 10.50	2.2 to 3.36	3.47 to 7.67	0.05 to 0.28	1.7 to 2.2	+AICRP, 1980—85 (unpublished)

Ref: *Nutrition Research cell, College of Home Science; APAU, Hyderabad.
+All India Co-ordinated Research Project, College of Home Scince, APAU, Hyderabad.

processing before consumption (*Wealth of India*, 1972; Pingale, 1973). Further investigation to find the nature of toxins present in the edible uncommon varieties grown by the tribals and the easier and quicker methods of reducing the toxicity is necessry.

Miscellaneous foods

Processed and dried tender bamboo shoots : The calcium, iron and phosphorus content of the bamboo shoots in the present study are 3 mg, 22 mg, 1049 mg per cent and the corresponding values reported by Pingale (1973) are 208 mg, 12.5 mg and 569 mg, respectively. Niacin content of the processed, dried bamboo shoots obtained in the present study has 0.03 mg per cent, which is quite low compared to 3.8 mg per cent reported by Pingale (1973). The differences in the mineral and vitamin content might be due to the pre-treatment given to the shoots before drying. In the present investigation, the shoots were shredded, boiled and dried whereas no such processing is reported by Pingale (1973). The young shoots are reported to contain a cyanogenic glucoside which is hydrolysed by an enzyme, also present in the shoots, when they are cut into pieces and soaked in water (*The Wealth of India*, 1948).

Dried mushroom: (*Agaricus sp.*) Proximate composition and vitamin content of dried mushroom is comparable to the values reported by Pingale (1973). However, the mineral content was variable.

Çaryota palm pith. The proximate principles and the vitamin content of caryota palm pith are comparable to the values reported by Pingale (1973). However, mineral content showed marked varitation as in the case of other foods. The iron content of palm pith is 51.7 mg and is high compared to the reported value of 1mg per cent by Pingale (1973) and Robson and Wadsworth, (1976). However, iron content of 22 mg per cent was reported by Gopalan *et al*(1980). Variations in the mineral content may be attributed to variety, location and soil conditions. However, to establish the utilitarian value of caryota palm pith, further investigation regarding its digestibility and nutrients is necessary.

Gingelly seed cake : It is a product much preferred by the tribals of the present study. It is a good complement to cereal/millet based diets. The iron content of the product (38.4 mg per 100 g) is double compared to the reported value (19.3 mg per cent) for gingelly seed cake (PAG, 1975). Though the mineral content of the product is higher its availablity is limited by the oxalates. However, they should be encouraged to prepare the same at home and also to increase the consumption for improving the quality of their diet.

Rajkeera seeds (*Amaranthus paniculatus*): It is a cereal like grain grown during May/June and harvested during October-November. The seeds contain high protein (16.8 g per cent). Earlier, several scientists also have reported similar protein content (Uzo and Okorie, 1983; Connor *et al*, 1980; Becker *et al*, (1981). It needs further investigation on the qualitative aspects in view of high protein and iron content.

Effect of processing on thiamine and niacin content

Tribals have a unique practice of leaving the left over rice and millets overnight in water drained, after cooking rice.

The practice of boiling cereals and millets in excess water and discarding the left over water resulted in a loss of 75 to 100 per cent thiamine (Table 2.25) and the loss is maximum with rice. The loss in thiamine may be attributed to its solubility and heat. Several scientists have reported similar findings. Rajyalakshmi (1981) reported a loss of 74.9 per cent thiamine in rice subjected to similar processing. Pushpamma *et al*, (1982) reported a loss of 36 to 83 per cent in cereal and millet products boiled for 10-45 minutes at 100°C. Aliya and Geervani (1981) reported a loss of 16-64 per cent on boiling of the millets bajra, jowar and ragi. As was pointed by Dwivedi and Arnold (1973) the type of processing, temperature, PH and the time of heating, presence of nitrites and sulphites might have contributed to the loss of thiamine in boiled cereals and millets. Contrary to this, thiamine content of the rice and jowar left overnight, increased by 36.3 to 66.6 per cent. But, in case of boiled bajra, *korra* and ragi products left overnight, such increase was not observed. The increase in thiamine may be due to fermentation of rice water in which rice is soaked. Hence, the practice of soaking cooked rice has nutritional advantage. However, no loss of thiamine is observed in case of cooked millets left overnight, hence it is not disadvantageous to keep boiled grain overnight.

Tribals have the practice of fermenting ragi batter for 15 to 18 hours with the addition of small quantity of bajra bran as a starter for initial fermentation. Though fermentation is reproted to have beneficial effect, cooking of fermented ragi batter is reported to result in loss of thiamine by 24 per cent (Aliya and Geervani, 1981). In the present study the per cent increase due to fermentation is not studied. However, the cooking of the fermented millet flour batter resulted in an increase in the thiamine content.

Loss of niacin (24 to 75 per cent) is found to be less than thiamine (75 to 100 per cent) due to boiling of rice and millets. It shows that niacin is more stable to heat processing. Pushpamma *et al* (1982), also reported a loss of niacin between 6 to 77 per cent in rice and millet products subjected to similar processing. However, overnight soaking of the cooked grain did not show an increase in niacin content as in the case of thiamine. But in case of fermented ragi product, an increase in niacin content by 36 per cent is seen. From these observations, it is seen that fermentation is advantageous in terms of improving B vitamin content of the product. Considering the total B-complex deficiency in the area, (Table 4.7) processes like malting, germination, and various combination products should be tried out and popularised in order to improve the quality of their diet.

Effect of processing on *in vitro* protein digestibility

Although the biological quality of proteins can be established only with feeding trials, the *in vitro* methods of protein evaluation being quick and inexpensive are useful in screening new protein foods. The pepsin-pancreatin index is reported to show a high correlation compared with *in vivo* data (r = 0.87) as tested with pepsin or pancreatin or pronase systems alone(Hahn *et al*, 1982; Buchmann, 1979; Akeson and Stahmann, 1964). Therefore the pepsin pancreatin digest index devised and advocated by Akeson and Stahmann (1964) is used in the present study for determining protein digestibility (*in vitro*). As major portion in the vegetarian diets is derived from cereals, millets and legumes, the digestibility of protein in these foods was evaluated.

Processing is found to reduce IVPD of cereals and millets from 43-97 per cent in the unprocessed, to 19-85 per cent in the processed ones, (Table 4.26) indicating a reduction in IVPD by 12 to 24 per cent due to boiling. Similar trend with experiments on sorghum was reported by Axtell *et al* (1981). They reported an IVPD of 78 to 100 per cent for the unprocessed sorghum and 45 to 55 per cent for the cooked one. However, no such gross differences were reported when tested *in vivo* on weaning rats (Axtell *et al*, 1981). Bradbury *et al*, (1984) also reported 11 per cent decrease in IVPD due to boiling of rice. The digestibility observed *in vivo* for rats may not be true for humans. However, *in vitro* digestibility studies may not be a reliable indicator of protein digestibility and may not be essentially similar with all cereals/millets. Maximum loss in IVPD (22 per cent) is noticed in combination product of bajra and rice followed by bajra gruel (2 per cent). The variations in IVPD of cereals/millets due to processing may be due to the differences in the solubilities of proteins as reported by Loranz and Dilsaver (1980)

Parboiling is a traditional practice among the rice eating population both in rural and urban areas in south India. Tribals not only parboil paddy but also parboil millets like *sama*, *ooda* and *korra* which is not the case in rural and urban areas. It is seen that reduction in IVPD due to parboiling is slightly more compared to raw grains. Kato *et al* (1983) indicated that during parboiling process, the unbound lipid and free fatty acid in millets and rice decreases whereas lipid bound to starch and protein and free phenolic acid increases, resulting in reduced extractability of protein. Perhaps, the extractability of protein made the difference in IVPD of parboiled and raw grain.

The reason for decrease in IVPD due to fermentation of ragi batter observed in the present study is not known. Whether same thing would happen *in vivo* also is not known. Studies on sorghum conducted by Axtell *et al* (1981) showed that fermentation has beneficial effect on protein digestibility as it provides partial digestion of proteins.

Roy (1984) in her study on sorghum reported that differences in processing like parching, popping, parboiling, and preparation of *roti* and biscuits showed no loss in IVPD as compared to whole grain. However, malting, germination and fermentation wre reported to have resulted in an increase of IVPD by 5 to 15 per cent (Axtell *et al*, 1981; Kazanas and Fields, 1981). Considering the major contribution of protein in the cereal/millet eating population in India, the possibility of preparing diverse food products with the processed coarse grains and their protein digestibilities should be further studied.

Contrary to the observation in cereals and millets, boiling of legumes improved the protein digestibility (*in vitro*). The values observed for unprocessed legumes are 40-72 per cent and processed ones showed 70-100 per cent indicating the improvement in IVPD by 15 to 32 per cent. The lowest IVPD value of 40 per cent is recorded for unprocessed *dukka chikkudu* (*Mucuna pruriens*) and field bean (black variety). With the other legumes the IVPD ranged from 62 to 73 per cent. In raw legumes, the presence of enzyme inhibitors such as trypsin, chymotrypsin are known to affect the protein digestibility which are found to be destroyed on cooking or some form of heat treatment resulting in an improvement in digestibility of proteins (Leiner, 1962; Kakada *et al*, 1969; E1Faki *et al*, 1984; Burr, 1975. Devadas *et al*, 1964; Singh and Jambunadhan, 1981; Rao *et al*, 1964; Deshpande *et al*, 1983; Subbulakshmi *et al*, 1976; Jambunadhan *et al*. 1981; Kuppuswamy *et al*, 1958; Elias *et al*, 1976).

The general health and living conditions of the tribals of the two agency blocks of Vizianagaram district are far from satisfactory. Though majority of the tribals are cultivators and can cultivate a variety of foods, the yield of many crops is low. The dietary situation of the tribals is not satisfactory as their diet mainly consists of cereals/millets and vegetables and lacks variety and bulk density. The diets of women and pre-school children are deficient in β-carotene, vitamin C, riboflavin, Calories and calcium and iron in children only. Inadequacy in the intake of calcium and iron which is not found in the diets of mothers but found in the diets of children is a clear indication of improper choice of foods for children. Some of their beliefs followed during lactation are irrational. Scabies/dermatitis, infection/infestation are found to be high which reflects poor health and sanitation in the area.

The cereals and millets grown in the area are mostly traditional varieties, and have low protein content compared to many improved varieties released by the research station located in the same district, and cultivated elsewhere in the state. Mineral content of the foods grown by tribals is generally high especially with varieties of ragi and horsegram. Some of their traditional food processing practices like fermentation, parboiling, soaking rice overnight are nutritionally beneficial. On the whole, the nutrient content of the foods consumed by tribals is comparatively lower. There has been no nutritional consideration in Agricultural planning in the tribal areas of Vizianagaram district. In spite of the potentiality to grow a variety of crops very little effort has been made to introduce new varieties, and horticulture has been a neglected area.

In terms of health facilities and services also tribals of Vizianagram district lag far behind the minimum requirements. Extension work through non-formal approach would have created awareness in the tribals about the basic needs of food, clothing, health, hygiene and water.

There is no organised marketing for the crops grown. Exploitation by middle-men is a common phenomenon leaving the tribals poorer in spite of producing some protective foods. No economic activity has been initiated, which is the root cause for depriving tribals of the forest and agriculture produce. Although there are educational facilities, it is only for children. Large number of women are ignorant of basic personal hygiene and child-care. Inadequate transfer of technology, and poor economic conditions are perhaps responsible for the present situation of tribals in Vizianagaram district of Andhra Pradesh.

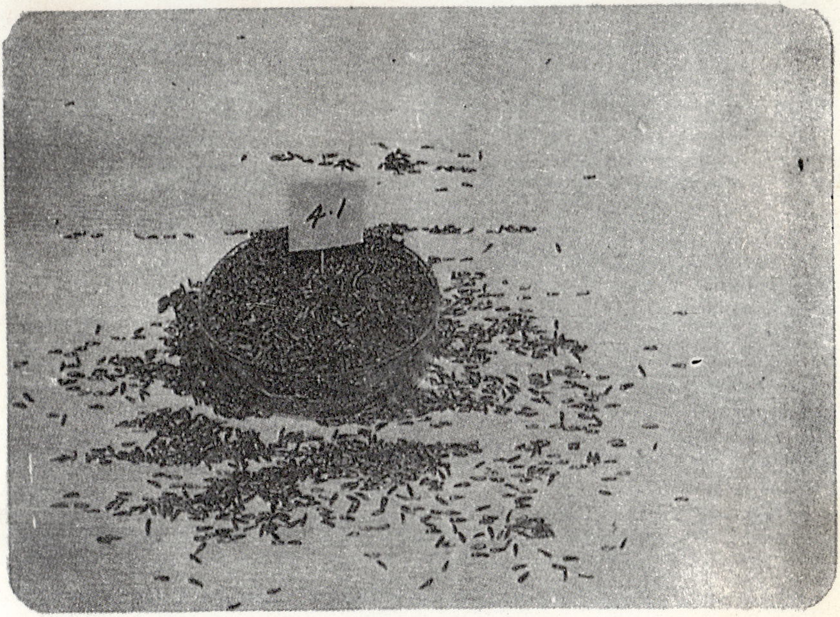

1. Olusulu (oilseed grown by Tribals)

2. *Dioscorea bulbifera*.

3. *Dioscorea hispida*.

4. Sinama Beans.

5. *Mucuna pruriens* (Dukka Chikkudu).

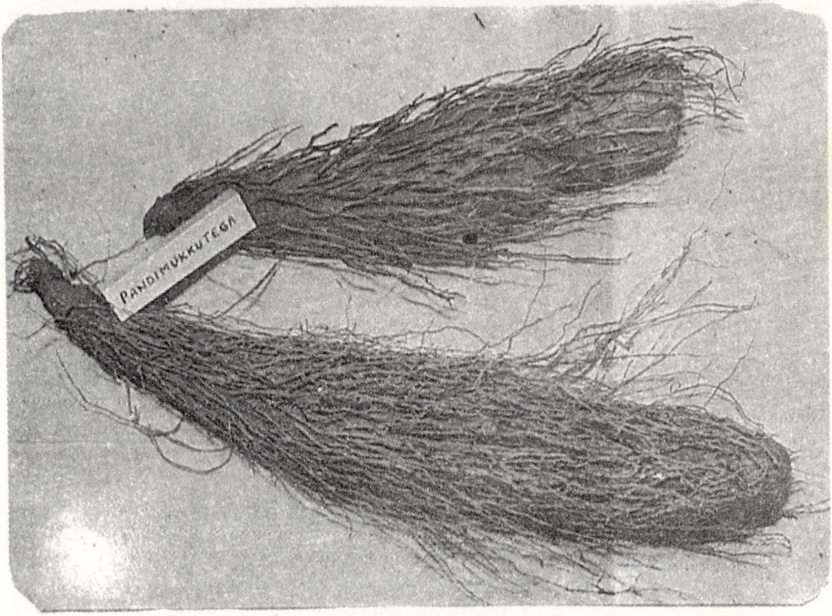

6. *Dioscorea pentaphylla*..

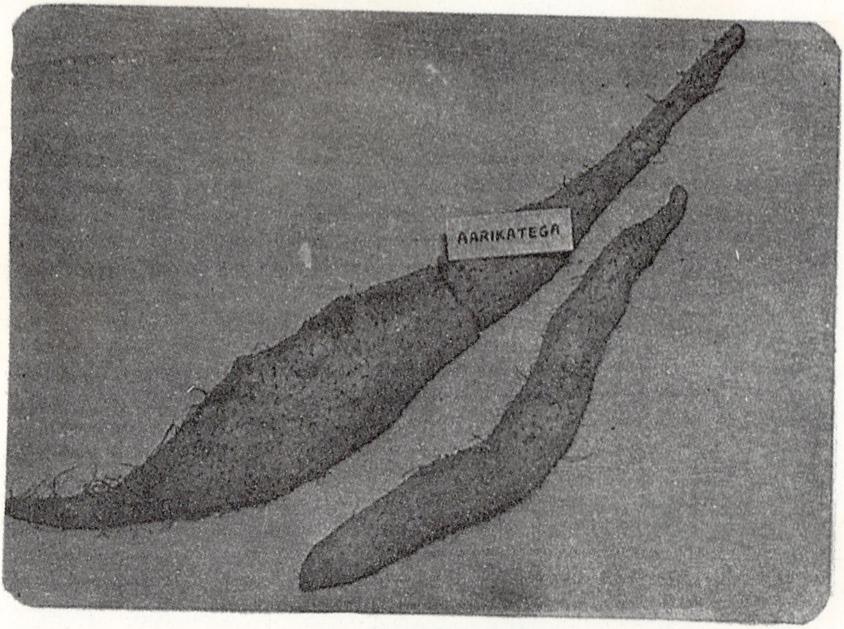

7. *Dioscorea oppositifolia.*

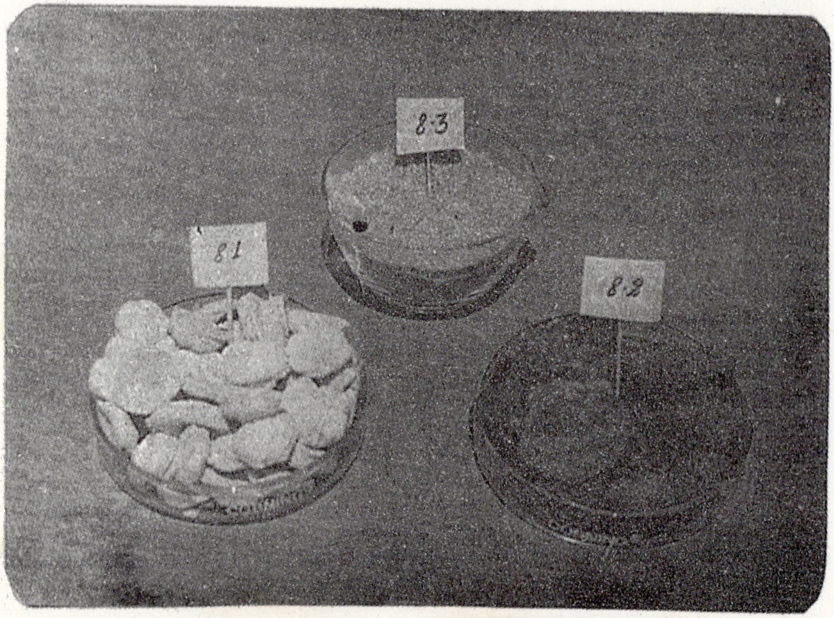

8. Prepared products used by the tribals.

9. Stored Products of the tribals.

10. Tribal women going to Shandy (market place).

11. A mother ready to go to fores.

12. A tribal mother with her children.

CHAPTER 6

CONCLUSION

There is always a significant variation in the living and dietary habits of tribals and non-tribal population. Tribals form 7.6 per cent of total population of India. Andhra Pradesh has the highest tribal population of 31.76 lakhs. The present study was carried in Vizianagaram district which has a tribal population of 1.53 lakhs. In Vizianagaram district two agency blocks selected are Bhadragiri and Pachipenta. Both these blocks have a total tribal population of 70,829. Considering the concentration of different tribes in these two blocks, four major tribes namely Jatapu, Savara tribes from Bhadragiri block, Gadaba and Kondadora from Pachipenta block were selected. In each tribe 75 households selected at random were covered for the study. Survey was carried out to collect information on demography and socio-economic conditions of tribals.

The foods cultivated by the tribals and the foods collected by the tribals from the forest for consumption was collected during September 1982 to March 1983. These foods were mainly cereals, millets, legumes, wild tubers and miscellaneous foods. These foods were analysed for proximate principles, vitamins and minerals. As tribals follow unique procedures in processing foods, all the common cereal/millet preparation of the tribals were prepared in the laboratory following exactly the same procedures adopted by the tribals, and analysed for nutrient composition. Some of the products were analysed for thiamine, niacin content and *in vitro* protein digestibility. A diet survey was conducted to assess the food and nutrient intake of women and pre-school children, in the tribal communities to assess the nutrient adequacy of the tribal populaiton. Information on morbidity pattern, infant feeding practices, food taboos was also collected.

The demographic structure of the tribal population reveals that the male to female sex ratio of the tribal populaiton is 1:1.03. The population of tribal children under 14 years of age group and below six years of age are less compared to all India average. The average family size is 4.63 and the dependency ratio is quite low being 26.5 per cent as compared to all India figures.

The morbidity pattern in the two blocks indicate a major incidence of scabies/dermatitis followed by infection and infestation. Incidence of B-complex deficiency and anacemia are 7 and 6 per cent, respectively. Only 3 per cent of eye diseases were of nutritional origin like bitot-spots, night-blindness and xerosis.

Agriculture is the major occupation of the tribals, and only 2 per cent were engaged in government jobs. Agricultural labour and collection of forest produce form the major economy with almost all the tribals. They cultivate diverse food crops. The major food crops grown include millets, legumes, oilseeds and other cash crops like turmeric, tabacco, ginger *etc*. The uncommon foods grown on hills are rajkeera seeds (*Amaranthus panciculatus*) and *dukka chikkudu* (*Mucuna pruriens*) *Judumulu* (*Vigna* sp.). Vegetables like gourds, pumpkin, brinjal and field beans are also grown. The main storage structures of the tribals are earthen-wares. Majority of the tribals stored staple grains for a period of 6 months or less. Among the wild foods stored round the year are mushrooms, tender bamboo shoots, caryota palm pith, mahuva seeds and mahuva flowers. Sun-drying is the common practice followed prior to storing of foods.

Millets are the staple foods of the tribals. Three meal pattern is common. Their diet is monotonous lacking variety and bulk density. Boiling is the common method adopted in processing of foods. It is usual practice to cook rice in combination with a millet and this formed the main dish. This is consumed with tamarind rasam/legume/spiced gingelly seed cake vegetables. Flesh foods excepting dry fish and cattle meat are rarely consumed.

The child feeding practices are poor. Majority of the women wean after 1 to 2 years. Children are weaned directly to an adult diet. No food restrictions are followed during pregnancy. However, severe food restrictions are followed during lactation and ill health. Several food fads and fallacies followed during lactation are found to be irrational.

The food intake of the woman indicated that consumption of cereals and other vegetables are adequate. Intake of flesh foods met 64% RDA and that of pulses/oil seed cake, green leafy vegetables and root vegetables, met 46 to 56 per cent RDA. The consumption of milk and milk products, fats and oilseeds, fruits, spices and condiments is nil. Energy requirement are met to the extent of 79 per cent RDA and the requirement of protein, calcium, iron, thiamine and niacin is adequately met. The diets are found to be deficient in β-carotene, vitamin C and riboflavin.

The deficit in food intake is considerable in the diets of pre-schoolers compared to women. The intake of cereals and vegetables is adequate, and that of pulses met 24 per cent and green leafy vegetables 11 per cent RDA. Intake of all other foods is grossly inadequate. The diets of the children are inadequate in all the nutrients. The requirement of calories met 56 per cent RDA, protein 74 per cent, thiamine 63 per cent and iron 66 per cent RDA. The diets are grossly deficient in β-carotene, vitamin C, riboflavin, calcium and niacin.

Nutrient analysis of various foods collected from the tribals indicate that the values with regard to proximate composition and vitamin content are mostly within the range of the reported values. The protein content of cereals/millets ranged from 6.8 g to 11.8 g per cent and that of legumes ranged from 20 to 27 g per 100 g. The protein content of cereals and millets cultivated by tribals is less compared to some of the improved varieties grown elsewhere in the state. *Dukka chikkudu* (a legume variety grown by tribals) has higher protein content and is consumed after special processing. The mineral content of the cereals/millets and legumes analysed is found to be somewhat higher as compared with other varieties grown in the state. The iron and calcium content of two ragi varieties and horsegram is found to be appreciably high.

Among the four wild tubers analysed *Pulidumpa* (*Dioscorea hispida*) has high protein content of 5.2 g per 100 g. The digestibility of starch (*in vitro*) in all the raw tubers is found to be less.

Among the four unconventional foods analysed, rajkeera seeds and dried mushroom are fair sources of protien. Dried mushrooms are rich sources of iron. Caryota palm pith and bamboo shoots are fair source of energy only.

Analysis of the nine cereal/millet products commonly consumed by the tribals showed that the cereal products kept soaked in rice gruel are higher in thiamine content. Ragi gruel, had a higher thiamine and niacin. The cooking time of cereals, more so of legumes is unusually long. The IVPD of cereal grains decreased by 9 to 24 per cent on cooking but IVPD of legumes increased by 40-73 per cent.

Suggestions

Setting up of extensive mobile health services is indispensable in order to provide timely medical facilities and help to the tribals living in interior areas.

Systematic epidemiological surveys should be conducted by health personnel to obtain a clear picture of morbidity and mortality in the tribal community.

As home deliveries are mostly practised by the community, training of local dayahs is essential.

Intensive health education campaign is essential for the prevention of communicable diseases.

Tribals should be encouraged to cultivate green leafy vegetables, papaya, and citrus fruits in their backyards. Active involvement of both the agriculturists and nutritionists is called for.

Production and consumption of pulses and oilseeds should be encouraged by providing facilities, proper incentives and technology.

As roots and tubers are an essential component of tribal diet, cultivation of nutritious roots like carrot, sweet potato, and potato should be encouraged in tribal areas.

Cultivation of some wild tubers like pulidumpa (*Dioscorea hispida*) should be taken up by agriculturists.

Maintenance of fresh water fish ponds should be encouraged by the tribals which helps in improving their nutrition and also socio-economic condition.

Government should organize better marketing facilities of foods grown or collected by tribals to prevent exploitation by non-tribals.

Cultivation and consumption of hybrid varieties of millets should be encouraged by proper motivation and alleviation of prejudices against the foods.

Agriculturists should explore the possibility of increasing the production of the two ragi (Tella and Punasa) and horsegram varieties cultivated by tribals which are rich in calcium.

Production of some uncommon legumes like Judumulu (*Vigna* sp.), and dukka chikkudu (*Mucuna pruriens*) a toxic legume, should be promoted as they contain high protein.

Further investigation should be taken up by the nutritionists to identify toxins in the foods and their removal by quick processing techniques.

Tribals should be weaned from podu cultivation by providing alternative arrangements for procurement of land, inputs and technology.

The practice of breast feeding the infants the same day after delivery is good and should be encouraged.

Nutrition education to mothers on proper weaning habits is indispensable as the children's diets are lacking both in quantity and quality.

Nutritionists should study the nutrition profile of the community.

Further investigation to confirm foods referred to as 'galactogogues' and having specific medicinal importance is needed.

Organization and maintenance of supplementary feeding programmes for the pre-school children and vulnerable mothers should be taken up by the Government as an immediate welfare measure.

Tribals should be persuaded to milk the cow and to consume milk and milk products especially by the children as their diets were found to be lacking in calcium.

Improved processing techniques should be taught to the tribals in order to minimise nutrient losses, cooking time and firewood.

Consumption of variety of millets should be encouraged by establishing fair price shops located in proximity.

Tribals should be discouraged from consumption of millets in gruel form which is found to be one of the reasons for calorie deficiency in their diets.

Some of their traditional cooking practices—parboiling of millets and paddy, use of millets and/or rice in combination , using fermented product and soaking left over rice in conjee and consuming the same as morning meal are found to be good in terms of nutritive value and should be encouraged.

Consumption of gingelly seed cake by the tribals should be encouraged in large quantities and methods of improving the quality should be extended.

Tribals should be encouraged and motivated to save money by introducing thrift programmes in order to save them from money-lenders.

Tribals should be persuaded to abstain from drinking alcohol.

Organization of non-formal education programmes should be taken up.

They should be made aware of various tribal welfare programmes implemented by the Government and should be helped to make use of the opportunities.

BIBLIOGRAPHY

Abdi, H. and K.M. Sahib. 1976. "Distribution of lysine in different legumes and some species of Amaranth seeds". *J. Food Sci. Tech.* 13:237-238.

Afolabi, O.A., O.L. Oke and I.B. Umoh. 1981. :"Preliminary studies on the nutritive value of some Cereal-like grains". *Nutr. Rep. Internat.* 24:389-394.

Akeson, W.R. and M.A. Stahmann. 1964. "A pepsin-pancreatin digest Index of protein quality evaluation". *J. Nutr. Dietet* 83:257-261.

Akpapunam, M.A. and P. Markakis. 1979. "Oligosaccharides of 13 American cultivers of cowpea (*Vigna sinesis*)". *J. Food Sci.* 4:1317-1318.

Al-Ani, M.R. 1980. "Diet and dietary habits of Nomads in Iraq". *Ecol. Food Nutr.*, 9:55-58.

Ali, A. 1978-79. "Health and Genetic problems of Kutia-Konds of Burlubaru village, Phulbani district (Orissa)". *Adibasi*, XVIII: pp. 56-62.

Aliya, S. and P. Geervani. 1981. "An assessment of the protein quality and vitamin B content of commonly used fermented products of legume and millets". *J. Sci. Food Agric.* 32:837-842.

Ambegaokar, S.D., S. Seshadri, H.C. Shah, V.P. Shinde, H.R. Adhikari, S.M. Patel and M.V.R. Rao. 1964. "Studies on the nutritive value of Indian Food stuffs 1. Proximate principles, minerals and vitamins". *J.Nutr. Dietet.* 1: 269-275.

AOAC, 1975. *Official and tentative methods of Association of Analytical Chemists.* 12th ed., The association, Washington, DC

Axtell, J.D., A.W. Kirleis, M.M. Hassen, N.D. Mason, E.T. Mertz and L. Munck, 1981," Digestibility of sorghum proteins". *Proc. Natl. Acad. Sci.* (U.S.A.) 78: 1333-1335.

Bailur, A. 1972. "Food Consumption patterns of pre-school children in India". In P.G. Tulpule., K.S. Jaya Rao (eds.). *Proceedings of the First Asian Congress of Nutrition*, 28 Jan-2 Feb. 1971. Nutrition Society of India, National Institute of Nutrition, Hyderabad.

Bailey, A.V., B. Piccolo, G. Sumrell and G. W. Burton. 1979. Aminoacid Profiles, chemical scores, and mineral contents of some pearl millet inbred lines. *J. Agric. Food Chem.* 27:1421-1423.

Baquar, S.R. and O.L. Oke. 1977. "Mineral Constituents of Nigerian Yams". *Nutr. Rep. Internat.* 15:265-272.

Battacharya, K.K., S.K. Biswas and J.K. Roy, 1972. "Studies on diet, body build and some aspects of infant nutrition. Kharwas of Palamau district in Bihar". *Bull. Anthrop. Survey India.* 21:69-72.

Becker, R., E.L. Wheeler, K. Lorenz, A.E. Stafford, O.K. Grosjean, A.A. Betschart and R. M. Saunders. 1981. "A compositional study of Amaranth grain". *J. Food Sci.* 46:1175-1180.

Beeson, K.C. and G. Matrone, eds. *The soil factor in Nutrition: Animal and Human*, 1976. vol. 2: Marcel Dekker, 1NC, New York and Basel. p. 32-34.

Benefice, E.S. Chevassus-Agnes and H. Barral. 1984. "Nutritional situation and seasonal variations for pastoralist populations of the Sahel (Senegalese Ferlo)" *Ecol. Food Nutr.* 14:229-247.

Berlin, E.A. and E.K. Markell. 1977. "An assessment of the Nutritional and health status of an Aguaruna Jivaro community, Amazonas, Peru." *Ecol. Food. Nutr.* 6:69-81.

Biellik, R.J. and P.L. Henderson. 1981. "Mortality, nutritional status and dietary conditions, in a food deficit region: North Teso district, Uganda", December, 1980. *Ecol. Food Nutr.* 11:163-170.

Bhowmik, K.L., S. Gupta, K.K. Chavdhari, M.K.P.Das and A. Bhowmik, eds 1971. *Tribal India : A Profile in Indian Ethnology*, The World Press Pvt. Ltd., Calcutta, p.1.

Bradbury, J.H., J.G. Collins and N.R. Pyliotis. 1984. "Digestibility of proteins of the histological components of cooked and raw rice". *Brit. J. Nutr.* 52:507-513.

Buchmann, N.B. 1979. "*In vitro* digestibility of protein from barley and other cereals". *J.Sci. Food Agric.* 30: 583-589.

Bureau of Economics and Statistics. 1981. *District Profile. Population and General Features, Vizianagaram.* Government of Andhra Pradesh, Hyderabad.

Bureau of Economics and Statistics, 1981-982. *Hand Book of Statistics*, Govt. of Andhra Pradesh, Hyderabad.

Burling, R. ed. 1965. *Hill farms and Paddy fields. Life in Main land South East Asia*. Prentice, Hall, 1NC. Englewood, p. 58-59.

Burr, K.H. 1975. Pulse Proteins. pp. 119-134. In M. Friedman (ed.). *Protein nutritional quality of foods and feeds*. part 2. Quality factors—plant breeding, composition, processing and antinutrients. vol. I. Marcel Dekker, 1NC. New York.

Calloway, D.H. and J.C. Gibbs. 1976. "*Food patterns and food assistance Programs in the Cocopah Indian community*". *Ecol. Food Nutr*. 5: 183-196.

Census of India. 1981. Series-2. "Provisional Population Totals", New Delhi, India.

Cerqueira, M.T., M.Mc Murry Fry and W.E. Connor, 1979, The food and nutrient intake of the Tara humara Indians of Mexico. *Amer J. Clin. Nutr*. 32:905-915.

Chatterjee,S.R. and Y.P. Abrol. 1975. "Aminoacid composition of new varieties of cereals and pulses and nutritional potential of cereal-pulse combinations" *J. Food Sci. Technol*. 12:221-227.

Chavan, J.K. and S.K. Duggal, 1978. "Studies on the essential aminoacid composition, protein fractions and biological value (BV) of some new varieties of rice". *J. Sci. Food Agric . 29:225-229.*

Cherian, A. 1981. "Attitudes and Practices of infant feeding in Zaria." Nigeria. *Eco. Food Nutr*. 2:75-80.

Chibber, B.A.K., E.T. Mertz and J.D. Axtell. 1980. *In vitro* digestibility of high tannin Sorghum at different stages of dehulling. *J. Agric.. Food Chem*. 28: 160-161.

Ciacco, C.F. and B.L. D'Appolonia. 1978. "Baking studies with cassava and yam flour 1. Biochemical composition of cassava and yam flour." *Cereal. Chem*. 55:402-411.

Connor, J.K., R.J.W. Gartner, B.N.Runge and Amos. 1981. "*Amaranthus edulis*: an ancient food source examined." *Nutr. Abst. and Rev*. 51c:3154.

Daspatnaik, P.S. 1976. "Liquor among the Dongria Konds of Orissa." *Adibasi*. XVI; 52-51.

DE Lumen, B.O. and L.A. Salamut 1980. "Trypsin inhibitor activity in winged bean (*psophocarpus tetragonolobus*) and the possible role of tannin." *J. Agric. Food Chem*. 28:533-536.

Deosthale, Y.G. and K.C. Pant. 1970. 'Nutrient composition of some red rice varieties." *Indian J. Nutr. Dietet. 7:283.*

Desthobe Y.G. and D.S.S. Rao. 1981. "Mineral and trace element composition of redgram (*Cajanus cajan*)." *Indian J. Nutr. Dietet.* 18: 130-135.

Deosthale Y.G., S. Devara, D.S.S. Rao and B. Belevady. 1979. "Effect of milling on mineral and trace element composition of raw and parboiled rice". *J. Sci. Food Agric.* 30:40-46.

Deosthale Y.G., V.S. Mohan and K.V. Rao. 1970. "Varietal differences in protein, lysine and leucine content of grain sorghum". *J. Agric. Food Chem.* 18:644-646.

Deosthale Y.G., V. Nagarajan and K.C. Pant. 1970. "Nutrient Composition of some varieties of ragi (*Eleusine corcana*)", *Indian J. Nutr. Dietet.* 7:80.

Deosthale Y.G., K.V. Rao, V. Nagarajan and K.C. Pant. 1971. "Varietal differences in protein and Aminoacids of grain bajra (*Pennisetum typhoides*)". *Indian J. Nutr. Dietet.* 8:301.

Deshpande, S.S., S.K. Sathe and M. Cheryan, 1983. *"In vitro* proteolytic digestibiltiy of dry bean (*Phaseolus vulgaris* L.) protein concentrates." *Nutr. Rep. Internat.* 27:931-936.

Devadas, R.P. and N.K. Murty. 1977. "Nutrition of the pre-school children in India, pp. 1-33. In G.H. Bourne (ed.) *Some aspects of Human nutrition. Nutrition of the pre-school children in India.* Wor. Rev. *Nutr. Dietet.* Kanger Basel, New York.

Devadas R.P., R. Leela and K.N. Chandrasekharan. 1964. Effect of cooking on the digestibility and nutritive value of the proteins of Blackgram (*Phaseolus mungo*) and green gram (*Phaseolus radiatus*). *Indian. J. Nutr. Dietet* 1:84-86.

Diva Sanjur. ed. 1982. *Social and cultural perspectives in Nutrition.* Hall. INC. Englewood Cliffs. pp. 172-174, 210.

Doggett, H. 1984. The improvement of nutritional quality by genetic mean. pp. 39-44. In K.T. Achaya, (ed.) *Interfaces between agriculture, nutrition and food science.* The United Nations University Press.

Dubois, M. K.A. Gilles, J.K. Hamilton, P.A. Rebers and F. Smith, 1956. Calorimetric method for determination of sugars and related substances. *Anal. Chem.* 28:350-356.

Dutta, L. and J.N. Barua 1978, "Evaluation of nutritional quality of some rice varieties grown in Assam", *Indian J. Nutr. Dietet* 15: 42-47.

Dwivedi, B.K. and R.G. Arnold. 1973., "Chemistry of B degradation in food products and model systems." *J. Agric. Food. Chem.* 21:54.

Ekpenyong, T.E. and R.L. Borchers. 1981, "Some toxic factors in inged bean seeds. 1. Anti trypsin hemagglutinating and urease activities." *Nutr. Rep. Internat.*23: 865-870.

ElFaki. H.A., L.V. Venkatraman and H.S.R. Desikachar. 1984, "Effect of processing on the *in vitro* digestibility of proteins and carbohydrates in some Indian legumes", *Qual. Plant. Plant Foods Hum nutr.* 34:127.

Elias, L.G., M. Hernander and R. Bressani,. 1976, "the nutritional value of precooked legume flours processed by different methods", *Nutr. Rep. Internat.* 14:385-403.

Elias L.G., M. Colindres and R. Bressani, 1964. "The nutritive value of eight varieties of cowpea (*Vigna sinesis)*", *J.Food Sci.* 29:118.

Fleuret, A. 1979, "The role of Wild foliage plants in the diet. A case study from Lushoto, Tanzania", *Ecol. Food Nutr.* 8:8-93.

Friedman, M. (ed.) 1975, Protein nutritional quality of foods and feeds part 2. Quality factors-plant breeding-composition processing and antinutrients. vol. 1.", Marcel Dekker, 1NC. New York. p. 119-134.

Giri, J., R. Parvatham and K. Santhini. 1981. "Effect of germination on the leaves of pectin, phytins and mineral, in three selected legumes.", *J.Nutr. Dietet.* 18:87-91.

Gopaldas, T., A. Gupta and K. Saxena. 1983, "The Phenomenon of sanskritization in a forest dwelling tribe of Gujarat, India: Nurtient intake and practices in the special groups", *Ecol.Food Nutr.* 13:1-18.

Gopalan, C., B.V. Ramasastri and S.C. Balasubramanian eds. 1980. "Nutritive value of Indian Foods", National Institute of Nutrition, Indian Council of Medical Research, Hyderabad. India.

Gore, A.P., T. Shobha and M. Kulkarni, 1977, "Nutritional status of tribes in the Indravati River Basin", *Indian J. Nutr. Dietet.* 14:167-171.

Goswamy, A.K. K.L. Sehgal and B.K.Gupta. 1970, "Chemical composition of bajra grains, 3. Indian Inbreds", *Indian J.Nutr,. Dietet.* 7:5-9.

Goswamy, A.K., K.L. Sehgal and K.P. Sharma. 1969, "Chemical Composition of bajra grains, 1. African varieties", *J.Nutr. Dietet.* 6:287-290.

Gramshaw, J.W. and F.A.O. Osinowo. 1982, "Volatile components of cooked tubers of the water yam (*Dioscorea alata)*", *J.Sci. Food Agric.* 33:71-80.

Greenhouse, R. 1981, "Preparation effect on iron and calcium in traditional pima foods," *Ecol. Food Nutr.* 10:221-225.

Grivetti, L.E. 1979, "Kalahari Agro-pastoral-Hunter-Gatherers: The Tswana example", *Eco. Food Nutr.* 7:235-256.

Gupta, B.M. and B. Bhandare. 1972, "Nutritional status of tribal and non-tribal rural pre-school children around Udaipur", *Ind. J. Paediatrics.* 39:317-326.

Gupta, B.M. and D.S. Wagle. 1978, "Antinutritional factors of phaseolus mungoreous (*Phaseolus mungo* var. M. IX, *Phaseolus aurevs* var-T_1)", *J. Food Sci. Technol.* 15:133-136.

Hahn, D.H., J.M., Fau Bion, G.H. Ring, C.A. Doherty and L.W. Rooney. 1982. "Semi-automated *in vitro* analysis of sorghum protein availability via pronase hydrolysis", *Cereal Chem.* 59:132-136.

Hawk, P.B., B.L. Oser and W.H. Summerson. eds. 1954. *Practical Physiological Chemistry* 12th ed. McGraw-Hill Book Company, 1NC. p 644.

Hoorweg, J. and R. Niemeyer. 1980, "Preliminary studies on some aspects of Kikuyu food habits", *Ecol. Food Nutr.* 9:139-150.

Horner, M.R., N.L. Stinton and D.J. Pringale, 1981, "Contributions of international food aid to diets of Nicaraguan children", *Ecol. Food Nutr.* 10:203-211.

Horner, M.R., W.S. Harris, B.J. Brownlees, R.S. Goldstein and A.K. Taylor. 1977, "Anthropometric and dietary study of Miskito Indian Children in rural Nicaragua", *Ecol. Food Nutr.* 6:137-146.

Hulse, J.H., M.L. Evangeline and E.P. Odette. eds. 1980, *Sorghum and the Millets*, Academic Press Inc. (London) Ltd. p. 740.

India, 1981, A Reference Annual. Publications Division, Ministry of Information and Broadcasting, Govt. of India, New Delhi.

Indian Council of Medical Research 1981, *Recommended dietary intakes for Indians*, New Delhi.

Jaffe, W.G., R. Moreno and V. Wallis. 1973, "Amylase inhibitors in legume seeds", *Nutr. Rep. Internat.* 7:169.

Jambunadhan, R., U. Singh and V. Subramanian. 1984, "Grain quality of sorghum, pearl millet, pigeon pea and chick pea." pp. 47-59. In Achaya (ed). *Interfaces between agriculture, nutrition and food science*. The United Nations University Press.

Joseph, F.G. 1981. "Commentary: Influence of development factors on nutritional patterns in the Solomon Islands". *Ecol. Food Nutr*. 10: 187-191.

Kadwe, R.S., K.K. Thakare and N.N. Badhe. 1974. "A note on the protein content and mineral composition of twenty five varieties of pulses". *Indian J. Nutr. Dietet.* 11:83.

Kakade, M.L., N. Simons and I.E. Liener, 1969, "An evaluation of natural vs. synthetic substrates for measuring the anti-tryptic activity of soybean samples", *Cereal Chem.* 46:518.

Kato, H. T. Ohta, T. Tsugita and Y. Hosaka. 1983. "Effect of parboiling on texture and flavour components of cooked rice", *J. Agric.Food Chem.*31: 318-823.

Kazanas. N. and M.L. Fields. 1981, "Nutritional improvement of sorghum by fermentation", *J. Food Sci.* 46:819-821.

Kon, S., J.R. Wagner, R. Becker, A.N. Booth and D.J. Robbins, 1971, "Optimizing nutrient availability of legume foods." *J. Food. Sci.* 36:635-639.

Kuhnlein, H.V. and D.H. Calloway, 1977, "Contemporary Hopi food intake patterns", *Ecol. Food Nutr.* 6:159-173.

Kurien, P.P. 1967a, "Nutritive value of refined ragi (*Elusine coracana*) Flour-1", J. Nutr. Dietet. 4: 96-99.

Kurien, P.P., 1967b, "Distribution of calcium and phosphorus between the husk and endosperm of rajgira seeds" (*Amaranthus paniculatus*)", *J.Nutr. Dietet.* 4: 152-154.

Kuppuswamy, S. M. Srinivasan and V. Subramanyan. eds. 1958. "Proteins in Foods Special report series No; 33", Indian Council of Medical Research. New Delhi, India pp. 35-60.

Kurtzman, R.H. 1975. "Mushrooms as a source of Food Protein pp. 305-318". In M. Friedman. (ed) *Protein Nutritional quality of foods and feeds Part* 2. Quality factors—plant breeding, composition, processing and antinutrients. vol. 1 Marcel Dekker, INC., New York.

Laurena, A.C., T.V. Den and E.M. Mendoza. 1984. "Effects of condensed tannins on the *in vitro* protein digestibility of cowpea *[Vigna unguicuita* (L) Walp}", *J. Agric. Food Chem.* 32: 1045-1048.

Lee, R.B. 1973, Mongongo, "the ethnography of a major wild food resource", *Ecol Food Nutr.* 2: 307-313.

Leiner, I.E. 1962. "Toxic factors in Edible legumes and their elimination", *Am. J. Clin. Nutr.* 11:281-284.

Leveille, G.A. 1972. "Modified thiochrome procedure for the determination of urinary thiamine", *Am. J. Clin. Nutr.* 25:273-274.

Longa, O.G. 1980. "Carbohydrate composition of different varieties of cowpea (*vigna unguiculata*)". *Food Chem.* 6: 153-161.

Lorenz, K.and G. Hinze. 1976. "Functional Characteristics of starches from proso and foxtail millets", *J. Agric. Food Chem.* 24: 911.

Lorenz, K., W. Dilsaver and L. Bates, 1980, Proso millets, Milling Characteristics, Proximate composition, Nutritive value of flours", *Cereal Chem.* 57:16-20.

Mallanna, K.N. and B.G. Rajashekara, 1969, "Hansa—a Protein rich high yielding white ragi, Mysore", *J. Agric. Sci.* 3:1-6.

Malleshi, N.G. and H.S.R. Desikachar, 1981 Research Note Varietal differences in Puffing quality of ragi". (*Eleusine coracana*). *J. Food Sci. Technol.* 18:30-31.

Manage, L. and K. Sohonie, 1972, "Proximate composition, aminoacid make up and *in vitro* proteolytic digestibility of horsegram.", *J. Food Sci. Tech.* 9;35.

Maxson. E.D., L.W. Rooney, R.W. Lewis, L.E. Clark and J.W. Johnson, 1973, "The relationship between tannin content, enzyme inhibition, rat performance and characteristics of sorghum grain", *Nutr. Rep. Internat.*8:145.

Meiners, C.R. N.L. Derise, H.C. Lau, S.J. Ritchey and E.W. Murphy, 1976a. "Proximate composition and yield of raw and cooked mature dry legumes", *J,. Agric. food Chem.* 24:1122-125.

Meiners, C.R. N.L. Derise, H.C. Lau, M.G. Crews, S.J. Ritchey and E.W. Murphy. 1976b. "The content of nine mineral elements in raw and cooked mature dry legumes", *J. Agric. Food Chem.* 24:1126-1130.

Monteiro, P.V., T.K. Virupaksha and D.R. Rao. 1982. "Proteins of Italian millet: aminoacid composition, solubility fractionation and electrophoresis of protein fractions", *J. Sci. Food Agric.* 33:1072—1079.

Morose, J.M., 1984, "Symposium of the cultural context of infant feeding in Fiji", *Ecol. Food Nutr.* 14:287-296.

Murthy, P.N.A.,J.M. Rao, S.B. Kadkol., K.S.K. Murthy, M.B. Rao, M.N. Satyanarayana and R.D. Thackare, 1965, "Nutritive Value of some Indian food stuffs", *Indian J. Med. Res.* 53:259-268.

National Institute of Nutrition. 1967. *Annual Report.*, Indian Council of Medical Research., Hyderabad, pp. 59-60.

National Institute of Nutrition. 1969. *Annual Report.*, Indian Council of Medical Research, Hyderabad, pp. 99-100.

National Institute of Nutrition. 1973. *Annual Report.*, Indian Council of Medical Research, Hyderabad, pp. 105-108.

National Institute of Nutrition. 1982. *Annual Report.*, Indian Council of Medical Research, Hyderabad, pp. 172.

National Institute of Nutrition 1983. *Annual Report.*, Indian Council of Medical Research, Hyderabad, pp. 199-200.

National Nutrition Monitoring Bureau, 1981. "Food and nutrient consumption pattern in the selected districts of different States 1980", National Institute of Nutrition, Indian Council of Medical Research, Hyderabad.

Newman, J.L. 1975, "Dimensions of Sandawe diet", *Ecol. Food. Nutr.* 4:33-39.

Oke, O.L. 1972, "Yam—A valuable source of food and drugs. p. 150-184" In G.H. Bourne (ed). *Worl. Rev. Nutr. Dietet. vol. 15*:Karger Basel.

Ologhobo, A.D. and B.L. Fetuga, 1983. "Investigations on the trypsin inhibitor, hemagglutinin, phytic acid and tannic acid contents of cowpea (*Vigna unguiculate)*", *Food Chem.* 12:249-254.

Ologhobo, A.D., and B.L. Fetuga, 1984. "Distributions of phosphorus and phytate in some Nigerian varieties of legumes and some effects of processing", *J. Food Sci.* 49:199-200.

Onuoha, G.B.I. 1982, "The changing scene of food habits and beliefs among the Mbaise people of Nigeria", *Ecol Food Nutr.* 11:245-250.

Opoku, A.R., S.O. Ohenhen and N. Ejiofor. 1981, "Nutrient composition of millet (*Pennisetum typhoides)* grains and malt". *Jr. Agric. Food Chem.* 29: 1247-1248.

Oria, H.F., M.M. Lima. and G.O. R. De 1975, Preliminary bromatological study of sorghum grain in Brazil, *Nutr. Abst. Rev.* 47:3825. p.444.

Osuhor, P.C. 1980, "Weaning practices amongst the Hausas", *J. Hum. Nutr.* 34 : 273-280.

Osuntogun, A.B., and O. Oke. 1983, "A note on the nutritive value of Amaranth seeds". *Food Chem.* 12:287-289.

PAG Compendium. 1975. Vol 2 World Mark Press Ltd. Halsted Press Division, John Wiley and Sons, New York. c. 1533.

Pingale, U.1973. "Some studies in two tribal groups of Central India. Part 1: Dietary intake and nutritional status", *Plant foods for man* 1; 185-194.

Pingle, U. 1973, Some studies in two tribal groups of Central India. Part 2, Nutritive importance of foods consumed in two different seasons. *Plant foods for man*, 1:195-208.

Pore, M.S. 1979, Proximate composition of horsegram varieties. *Indian, J. Agric. Sci.* 49:532-534.

Pore, M.S., and N.G. Magar, 1977 Nutritive value of hybrid varieties of finger millet. *Indian J. Agric. Sci.* 47:226-228.

Pratap, D.R., 1975. *Tribes of Andhra Pradesh.* World Telugu conference publication. 1st world Telugu conference office, Hyderabad, India, pp. 1-63.

Pratap, D.R. 1973, "the dietary habits and nutritional status of Chenchus",

Tribal Cultural Research and Training Centre. Tribal Welfare Dept. Hyderabad. Government of Andhra Pradesh.

Pushpamma, P. and K.C. Rao. eds. 1981. "Varietal preference, Marketing, storage, processing and utilizaiton of sorghum and millets in Andhra Pradesh." College of HomeScience, Andhra Pradesh Agricultural University, Hyderabad, India.

Pushpamma, P., P. Geervani and K.K. Kumari, 1982, "Losses of some nutrients in cereal, millet and legume recipes commonly consumed in Andhra Pradesh. *Indian. J. Nutr. Dietet.* 19:342—349.

Pushpamma, P., K.C. Rao and R. Tulpule, 1983, Profile of tribal families in East Godavari District, ITDA Report, College of Home Science, Andhra Pradesh Agricultural University, Hyderabad.

Pushpamma, P., K.C. Rao., P. Rajyalkshmi and K.K. Rao. 1983. "Household processing of legumes in Andhra Pradesh, India", *Legume Research.* 6:1-8.

Rajalakshmi, R.ed. 1981, *Applied Nutrition.* 3rd edition. Oxford and I.B.H. Publishing Co. New Delhi, India. p. 165.

Ramasastry, B.V. 1976. A simple method for Estimation of Thiamine in Foods using Base-Exchange on sand instead of Decalso. *Internat. J. Vit. Nutr. Res.* 46:403-411.

Ramachandra, G., T.K. Virupaksha and M. Shadakharaswamy, 1977. "Relationship between tannin levels and *in vitro* protein digestibility in finger millet (*Eleucine coracana* Gaerthn)". *J. Agric. Food Chem.* 25: 1101-1104.

Randall., E. and D.Sanjur, 1981, "Food preferences, their conceptualization and relationship to consumption". *Ecol. Food Nutr.* 11:151-161.

Rao, D.H. 1971,"The tribal diets," *Nutrition,* A quarterly Publication of the National Institute of Nutrition, Indian Council of Medical Research Hyderabad. 6:2-9.

Rao, D.H. and K. Satyanarayana. 1974, "Nutritional Status of tribal pre-school children of Andhra Pradesh", *Indian J. Nutr. Dietet.* 11:328-334.

Rao, P.U. and B. Belavedy, 1979, "Chemical composition of high yielding varieties of pulses, varietal, locational and year to year differences", *Indian J. Nutr. Dietet.* 16:440-446.

Rao, D.S.S. and Y.C, Deosthale. 1980, "Effect of pearling on mineral and trace element composition and ionisable iron content of sorghum", *Nutr. Rep. Internat.* 22: 723-728.

Rao, S.V., R. Leela, M. Swaminathan and H.A.B. Parpia, 1964, "The nutritive value of leguminous seeds," *Indian. J. Nutr. Dietet.* 1:304-321.

Ray, P.K. 1971, "Nutritive value of Horsegram (*Dolichos biflorus*).111. "Determination of biological value, digestibility and net protein utilization" *Indian. J. Nutr. Dietet.* 7:71.

Robson, J.R.K. and G.R. Wadsworth. 1977, "The health and nutritional status of primitive population", *Ecol. Food Nutr.* 6:187-202.

Robson, J.R.K., D.E. Yen and B.P.B. Museum 1976, "Some nutritional aspects of the Philippine Tasaday diet", *Ecol. Food Nutr. 5:83-89.*

Roy, J.K. 1976, "Economic background, dietary habits and nutritive value of the diet of Khonds in Koraput distict of Orissa". *Bull. Anthrop. Survey India,* 19:75-96.

Roy, S. 1984, "Protein and energy availability of processed sorghum products". Ph.D. thesis, Department of Food and Nutrition, College of Home Science, APAU, Hyderabad.

Roy, S.K. and A.K. Rao, 1957, "Investigations on the diets of Murias of Bastar district", *Bull. Dept. Anthrop.* 6:33-45.

Roy, S.K. and R.K. Rao,. 1962, "Diets of some Indian Tribes", *Indian J. Med. Res.* 59:905-914.

Salimath, P.V. and R. N. Tharanathan, 1982. "Carbohydrates of field bean (*Dolichos lablab*)" *Cereal Chem. 59:430-435.*

Satwadhar. P.N., S.S. Kadam. and D.K. Salunkhe. 1981. "Effect of germination and cooking on polyphenols and *in vitro* protein digestibility of horsegram and mothbean." Qual,. Plant. Plant foods Hum. Nutr. 31:71-76.

Sawaya,. W.W., J.K. Khalil and W.J. Safi. 1984. "Nutritional quality of pearl millet flour and bread", Qual. Plant. Plant Foods Hum. Nutr. 36:117.

Sen Gupta, P.N. 1960, "Dietaries of Primitive tribes", *The Adibasis,* Revised Ed. Publications Division, Delhi. pp. 87-95.

Sen Gupta, P.N. 1980, "Food consumption and nutrition of regional tribes of India, *Ecol,"*. *Food Nutr*. 9:93-108.

Sen Gupta, P.N. and S.K. Biswas. 1956, "Studies on the diet and nutritional status of the Kanikkar and Urali tribes of Travancore", *Bull. Dept. Anthropl*. 5:43-52.

Sharma. K. ed. 1971. *The Konds of Orissa* (An Anthropometric study) Concept publishing company. New Delhi pp. 27-43.

Sharma. Y.K., A.S. Tiwari and A. Mishra. 1977, "Studies on chemical constituents and their influence on cookability in pigeonpea." *J. Food Sci. Technol*. 14;33-40.

Shehata. S.A.Y. and A.M. Thannoun. 1981. Chemical and aminoacid composition of Iraqi mung beans. *Nutr. Abst. Rev. Series* A. 51:6996.

Shehata. S.A.Y. and A.M. Thannoun. 1983, "Chemical and Aminoacid composition of Iraqi mung beans" *Food Technol. Abst*. 189:2008.

Shobhana., P.S. Sangawan, H.S. Nainawatee and B.M. Lal. 1976. "Chemical composition of some improved varieties of pulses". *J. Food. Sci. Technol. 13;49-51*.

Singh, V. and R. Jambunathan. 1978, "Studies on Desi and Kabuli Chickpea (*Cicer arietinum* L.) cultivars: Levels of protease inhibitors, levels of polyphenolic compounds and *in vitro* protein digestibilty" *J. Food Sci. 46:1364-1367*.

Singh, V. and R. Jambunathan 1981. Protease inhibitors and *in vitro* protein digestibility of pigeonpea {*Cajanus cajan (L) Mill* sp}. and its wild relatives. *Food Sci. Technol. 18:246-247*.

Singh V., K.C. Jain, R. Jambunathan and D.G. Fairs 1984. Nutritional quality of vegetable pigeonpea (*Cajanus cajan* (L), Mill sp.) : Dry matter accumulation, carbohydrates and proteins. *J. Food Sc*.49 : 779-802.

Singh. L. N., Singh. M.P. Shrivastava and A.K. Gupta. 1977, Characteristics and utilization of vegetable types of pigeonpeas (*Cajanus cajan* (L) Mill sp.). *Indian J. Nutr. Dietet*. 14:8-10.

Snedecor, G.W. and W.G. Cochran. eds. 1967, *Statistical Methods*. 6th Edition,. Oxford and IBH. Publishing Co. New Delhi. 258-268.

Soaad, H., Al-Bayati and H. Al-Rayess. 1981, "The chemical composition of Iraqi rice and rice by-products. *J. Food. Sci. Technol*. 18:40-43.

Srihara. P. 1976, "The nutritive composition of 'Hebbal a vare' is comparable to local varieties". *Current Research* 5: 95-96.

Srikantia, S.G. 1984, "Interactions between Nutrition and agriculture in India", pp. 352-362. *In* K.T. Achayya (Ed) *Interfaces between agriculture nutrition and food sciences.* The United Nations University Press.

Subbulakshmi, G., K.G. Kumar and L.V. Venkataram, 1976, "Effect of germination on the carbohydrates, proteins, trypsin inhibitor, amylase inhibitors and hemagglutinin in horsegram and moth-bean", *Nutr. Rep. Internat.* 13:19-31.

Subharani. S. 1984, "Nutritional status of tribal pregnant and lactating women and effect of supplementary feeding on pre-schoolers", Vizianagaram district , Andhra Pradesh. M.Sc. Thesis, Department of Foods and Nutriiton, College of Home Science, APAU. Hyderabad.

Swain, E.W., H.L. Wang and C.W. Hefseltine, 1978, "Note on vitamin and minerals of wild rice", Cereal Chem. 55:412-414.

Swaminathan, M.C., D.K.L. Iyengar and D.H. Iyengar and D.H. Rao, 1971, "Health Survey of the Onge tribe of little Andamans". *Indian J. Med. Res.* 59:1136-1147.

Taira, H. 1971, "Protein content of uplaid rice grains", *Nutr. Abst. Rev.* 41:268.

Thomson, W.S. and D.T. Lewis, eds, 1980, "*Population Problem.* Chapter 5. Age and sex composition of population", 5th Edition, Tata McGraw-Hill Publishing Company Ltd., New Delhi. pp. 73-113.

The Wealth of India Raw Materials, 1984, Publication and Information Directorate, Council of Scientific and Industrial Research. Govt. of India, New Delhi 1:153-154.

The Wealth & India Raw Materials, 1962. A dictionary of Indian raw materials and Industrial products. Publication and information directorate, Council of Scientific Industrial Research,Govt. of India, New Delhi. 3:442-433.

Tribal Cultural and Training Institute, 1969, "Survey of tribal development block. Bhadragiri, Srikakulam District. Series 3," Tribal welfare Departement, Hyderabad. Government. of Andhra Pradesh.

Udipi, S. and B.D. Punekar, 1980, "Nutritive value of mushrooms", *Indian J. Med. Res.* 72:241-244.

UNICEF, 1984, "An analysis of the situation of children in India". Regional Office for South East Asia, New Delhi, India.

Uzo, J.O. and A.U. Okarie, 1983, "Amaranthus Hybridus: a potential grain crop for West Africa", *Nutr. Rep. Internat.* 27:519-524.

Van Steenbergen, W.M., J.A. Kusin., H.J. Nordbeck, and A.A.J. Jansen, 1984, "Food consumption of different household members in Machkos, Kenya", *Ecol. Food Nutr.* 14:1-9.

Varriano-Martson E. and R.C. Hoseney. 1980, Note on mineral content and location in pearl millet", *Cereal Chem.* 57:150-152.

Vasi, I.G. and G.M. Desai. 1976, *"In vitro* digestibility of proteins present in some cereals and pulses grown in South Gujarat," Science and culture, 42:126-128.

Vaughan, D.A., M. Womack., R.T. Smith. and W.J. Wiser, 1980. "Protein quality of rice as affected by application of nitrogen fertilizer", *J. Agric. Food Chem.* 28:894-896.

Vidyarthi. L.P. 1973-74. "Strategy for tribal development in India", *Adibasi*, 15:77-79.

Viswanath, J.K. and G.N. Gajanan, 1979, "Nutritive value of foxtail millet", *Current Research* 8:52-53.

Wahid, M. T. Hussain and R. Baksh, 1975, "Aminoacid composition and Nutritive value of rice varieties Basmati-370 and 1R-6 grown in Peshawar region", *J. Sci. Ind. Res.* 18:51-53.

Wankhede, D.B. A. Shehnaj and M.R. Rao 1979, "Carbohydrate composition of finger millet (*Eleusine coracana*) and foxtail millet. (*Setaria italica*)", *Qual. Plant. Plant Foods Hum. Nutr.* 28:293-303.

Watson, J.D. 1977. "Chemical composition of some less commonly used legumes in Ghana", *Food Chem.* 2:267-271.

Webster. J., W. Beck and B. Ternai. 1984, "Toxicity and bitterness in Australian *Dioscorea bulbifera* L. and *Dioscorea hispida* Dennst. from Thailand", *J. Agric. Food Chem.* 32;1087-1090.

Weiwo, C.K. and H.H. Draper, 1975, "Vitamin E status of Alaskan Eskimos", *Amer J. Clin. Nutr.* 28:808-813.

Will, R.B.H., K.B. Palipane and H. Greenfield, 1983, "Composition of Australian Foods", *Nutr. Abst. Rev. Series* A 53:189.

World Health Organization, 1981, "Development of indicators for monitoring progress towards health for all by the year 1981, Geneva", p. 79.

Appendix

A SCHEDULE TO INVESTIGATE THE FOOD HABITS OF THE TRIBALS OF VIZIANAGARAM DIST. (A.P.)

1.1 Family No. :

1.2 Date :

1.3 Block :

1.4 Village :

2.1 Name of the Head of the household :

2.3 Occupation :

Main :

Subsidiary :

2.4 Family particulars :

Name of the family member	Sex	Age

3.1 Food availability :

Name of the foods available	Source	Period of Availability	Used for regular consumption Yes=1: No = 0
Cereals:			
Legumes:			
Vegetables:			
Roots:			
Leafy Vegetables:			
Fruits			
Any Other			

Source: 1. Own
2. Shandy
3. Local Shops
4. Girijan Stores
5. Any other

3.2 Food storage :

Food Stored	Place of Storage	STORED From	STORED Quantity	STORED Period	Pre-treatment given
Cereals					
Legumes					
Vegetables					
Roots					
Leafy Vegetables					
Fruits					
Any Other					

3.3 Family meal pattern:

Meal of the day	Pattern
Breakfast	
Lunch	
Dinner	
In Between Meals	

3.4 Dietary Intake:

Meal of the day	Total Quantity (g)		Quantity Consumed (G)	
	Raw	Cooked	By women	Pre-School Children
Breakfast				
Lunch				
Dinner				
In Between Meals				

3.5 Food Fads:

a) Which foods do you believe to be good for health :

NAME OF THE FOOD

____

____

____

____

____

b) Which are the foods you believe to be not good for health.

NAME OF THE FOOD

____

____

____

____

____

____

4) Consumption practices :

Name of the food/ preparation	Frequency consumed	INGREDIENTS USED				PROCEDURE	CONSUMPTION
		MAJOR	QTY. (G)	MINOR	QTY(G)		

2) FREQUENCY :
1) Daily
2) Weekly-Thrice
3) Weekly-Once
4) Twice a month

8. CONSUMPTION
1) Consumed immediately
2) Stored and taken during the whole day.

5) What special foods/preparation do you give for the following

Group	Preferred Foods	Preferred Preparation
Pregnant Women		
Lactating Women		
Infants at Weaning Stage (6-12 Months)		
Pre-School Children (1-6 Years)		
Fever		
Diarrhoea		
Respiratory Infections		
Any Other		

INDEX

G

H

I

J

L

M

N